Dear Friend,

The thrill we experienced at Pillsbury with our first sampling of these prize-winning recipes is waiting for you when you taste these dishes created by America's best cooks for the Bake-Off.

When it comes to your actual baking, we know you'll enjoy the results. Every recipe has been tested and adapted in the Ann Pillsbury kitchens for perfect baking every time.

We know you'll want to use the same fine ingredients the prize winners used.

When it comes to flour, years of experience have produced Pillsbury's BEST ... the fine, light, fluffy flour that adds so much to the joy of creative baking.

Pillsbury's BEST has become a tradition in countless households. Try it soon in your baking.

Sincerely,

Ann Pillsbury

P.S. Would you like to share your favorite recipe with us? It could take you to next year's Bake-Off. You'll find an entry blank in this booklet.

This is the Bake-Off—

—flavored with excitement from the moment finalists are notified they're going. Tours and parties planned are on the agenda for their big weekend. And in the International Ballroom of the Beverly Hilton Hotel await 100 ranges and kitchen counters, marked by state and supplied with four times the makings for every recipe. On Bake-Off morning, finalists form up to march into the "world's biggest kitchen." Television camera lights go up, flash bulbs pop, hometown newspaper food editors stop by the ranges for the stories on their contestants, and Bake-Off master of ceremonies Art Linkletter does television interviews for tomorrow's program. Even with all this to-do, jittery nerves grow calm as finalists go through the familiar baking steps —some find time to read while rolls rise or cakes are in the oven— others exchange samples of their baking, chat, have a cup of coffee. Hotel bus boys whisk away dirty dishes and mixing bowls, bring them back sparkling clean. Bake-Off officials stand by to smooth any problems.

Soon finished entries begin to go into the guarded room where 11 food editors and broadcasters sit on the judge's panel. Breakfast in bed traditionally starts the next day but the big meal is luncheon —the Awards Luncheon, prefaced by the Awards program and telecast— with the name of the Grand prize winner announced by Art Linkletter, and her $25,000 check presented by Guest of Honor, Mrs. Edmund G. Brown, wife of California's governor. Nobody's going home a loser—everyone wins a new range and mixer, $100, and the trip to the Bake-Off. Tomorrow they'll all be home—with quite a story to tell their families. Tomorrow the Bake-Off will be over—for this year. But pleasant memories will linger for a long time to come.

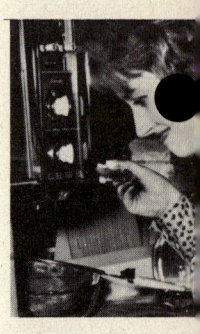

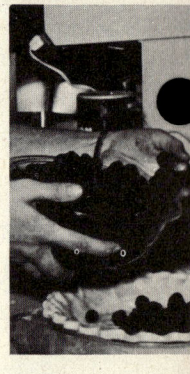

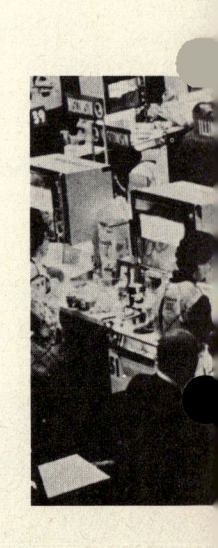

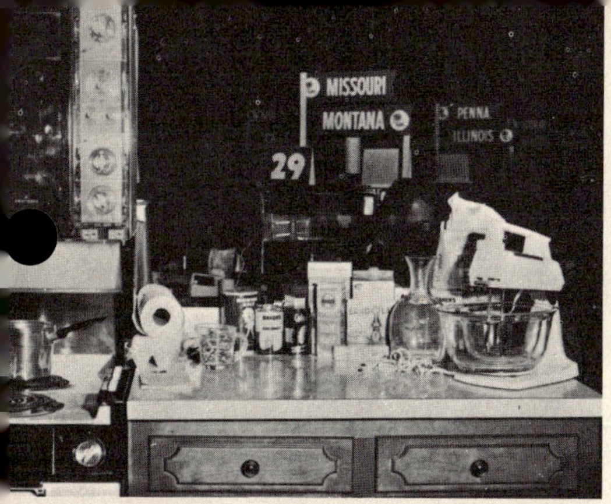
MISSOURI
MONTANA
PENNA
ILLINOIS
29

Pillsbury's
BEST
XXXX

NEW MEXICO
HAWAII
OREGON
OHIO
COLO
ILLINOIS
WASHINGTON
20
19
11
12
5

Pillsbury's
BEST
XXXX
Pillsbury's
BEST
XXXX
FLOUR

Pillsbury's
15th
AKE-OFF

Feels different
More granular than powdery. No dust. Pours like sugar so you never need to sift.

Acts different
Blends instantly in cold liquids, so gravies and sauces will always be smooth.

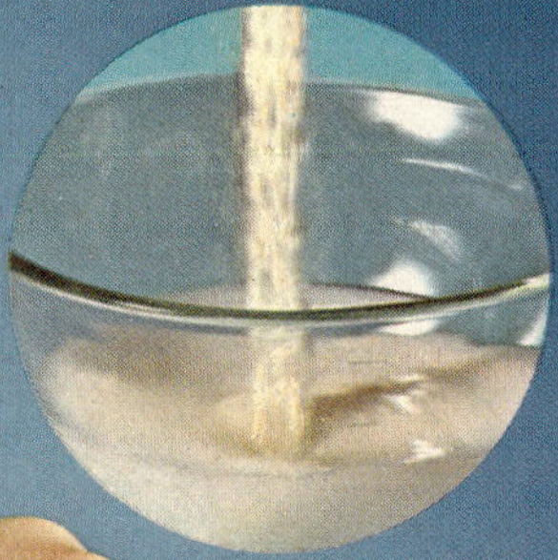

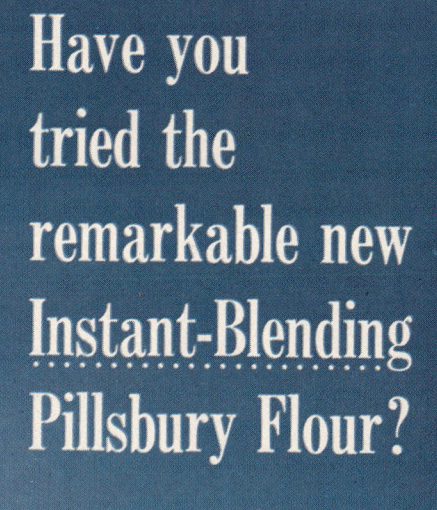

Looks different
Only Pillsbury has this new bag. An instant-opening top with its own handy pour spout.

Have you tried the remarkable new Instant-Blending Pillsbury Flour?

Truly an All Purpose Flour

You'll bake your proudest cakes and cookies... your flakiest pies and biscuits ... your springiest rolls and breads. Quicker and easier, too than you've ever baked before.

This is the new flour that opens in an instant, pours in an instant, blends in an instant. Try it—for a rewarding new experience in baking.

PAGE 6 | MAIN DISHES

A part-time poet, Mrs. Roman Walilko of Detroit is a full-time homemaker for her industrial engineer husband and their five children—whose hearty appetites had a lot to do with the creation of her $25,000 Grand Prize Winning casserole.

MAIN DISHES | PAGE 7

To save last minute time, prepare meat mixture ahead. Refrigerate. Just before dinner, reheat then top with biscuits and bake.

Hungry Boys' Casserole

$25,000 Grand Prize Winner by Mrs. Roman Walilko, Detroit, Michigan

BAKE at 425° for 25 to 30 minutes. SERVES 6 to 8.
(MAKES 12x8-inch casserole.)

Sauté......... in large skillet
    1½ pounds **ground beef**
    1 cup sliced **celery**
    ½ cup chopped **onion**
    ½ cup chopped **green pepper** and
    1 **clove garlic**, minced, until vegetables are tender; drain.

Add.......... ¾ cup (6-oz. can) **tomato paste**
    ¾ cup **water**
    ½ teaspoon **monosodium glutamate**
    1 teaspoon **salt** and
    1 teaspoon **paprika**. Reserve 1 cup for Biscuits.

Add.......... 1 can (1 lb.) **Campbell's Pork and Beans**, undrained, and
    1 can (1 lb.) **chick peas** or **lima beans**, undrained. Simmer while preparing Biscuits.

Biscuits

Sift together... into mixing bowl
    1½ cups sifted **Pillsbury's Best All Purpose Flour***
    2 teaspoons double-acting **baking powder**
    ½ teaspoon **salt**

Cut in........ ¼ cup **Land O'Lakes Butter** until particles are fine.

Combine...... ½ cup **milk** and
    4 drops **Burnett's Yellow Food Coloring**, if desired. Add to flour mixture. Stir until dough clings together.

Knead........ on floured surface 12 times. Roll out to a 12x9-inch rectangle.

Combine...... ½ cup sliced **pimiento-stuffed olives**
    ¼ cup blanched slivered **almonds** and the reserved meat mixture. Spread over dough. Roll up, starting with 12-inch side; seal edge. Cut into 1-inch pieces.

Turn.......... meat mixture into 12x8 or 13x9-inch baking dish or a 11-inch round casserole. Top with biscuits.

Bake......... at 425° for 25 to 30 minutes until golden brown.

**For use with Pillsbury's Best Self-Rising Flour, omit baking powder and salt.*

MAIN DISHES

Pork or ground beef may be substituted for veal.

Venetian Veal Pie

Senior Third Prize Winner by Mrs. Kennett C. Johnson, St. Louis, Missouri

BAKE at 400° for 30 to 35 minutes. SERVES 6.
(Makes 9-inch pie.)

Sift together... 1½ cups sifted **Pillsbury's Best All Purpose Flour*** and
1 teaspoon **garlic salt** into mixing bowl. Add
1 teaspoon **leaf oregano** and
¼ cup grated **Parmesan or Romano cheese.**

Cut in....... ½ cup **Land O'Lakes Butter** or other shortening until particles are fine.

Sprinkle...... 4 to 5 tablespoons cold **water** over mixture while stirring with fork. Add water to driest particles, pushing lumps to side, until dough is moist enough to hold together.

Roll out...... two-thirds of dough on floured surface to a circle 1½ inches larger than inverted 9-inch piepan. Fit into pan.

Meat Filling

Coat......... 1 pound **veal steak,** cut in bite-size pieces, with
½ cup **flour.** Brown meat in
¼ cup **Land O'Lakes Butter** or cooking oil in large skillet, using all the flour.

Add.......... 2 cups (1-lb. can) **tomatoes**
1 cup (8-oz. can) **tomato sauce**
¼ cup chopped **onion**
3 tablespoons grated **Parmesan or Romano cheese**
1 tablespoon **sugar**
1 teaspoon **sweet basil**
½ teaspoon **salt**
½ teaspoon **garlic salt**
½ teaspoon **leaf oregano** and
⅛ teaspoon **pepper;** mix thoroughly. Cover; simmer 30 minutes or until meat is tender.

Turn......... into pastry-lined pan. Top with
4 slices (¼ lb.) **Cheddar or Brick cheese.**

Roll out...... remaining dough to ⅛ inch. Cut into rounds with 2-inch cutter. Place over cheese, overlapping slightly. Fold edge to form a standing rim; flute.

Bake......... at 400° for 30 to 35 minutes until golden brown.

**Pillsbury's Best Self-Rising Flour may be substituted.*

MAIN DISHES | PAGE 9

Three cups leftover pork roast may be substituted for the pork shoulder.

Party Pork Barbecue

Senior Winner by Mrs. C. E. Yearling, Payne, Ohio

BAKE at 400° for 20 to 25 minutes.   SERVES 6 to 8.
(Makes 2-qt. casserole.)

Combine...... ¼ cup **Pillsbury's Best All Purpose Flour**
½ teaspoon **salt** and
⅛ teaspoon **pepper**.

Coat......... 1½ pounds boneless **pork shoulder**, cut in bite-size pieces, with flour mixture. Brown well in
3 tablespoons **cooking oil** or shortening in large skillet.

Add.......... 1½ cups chopped **celery**
1 medium **onion**, sliced and broken into rings
1 cup (8-oz. can) undrained **pineapple tidbits**
1 cup **catsup**
½ cup **water**
2 tablespoons chopped **green pepper**
2 tablespoons prepared **mustard**
1 tablespoon **Worcestershire sauce** and
1 teaspoon **salt**. Cover; simmer 20 to 30 minutes or until meat is tender.

Turn......... into 2-quart casserole.

Drop Biscuits

Sift together... into mixing bowl
1 cup sifted **Pillsbury's Best All Purpose Flour***
1½ teaspoons double-acting **baking powder**
½ teaspoon **salt**
½ teaspoon **celery salt**

Cut in........ ¼ cup **shortening** until particles are fine.

Add.......... ⅓ cup **milk**
1 slightly beaten **egg**
1 tablespoon dry **onion flakes** and
2 tablespoons **mushrooms**, chopped, if desired. Stir only until all dry particles are moistened.

Drop......... by rounded tablespoonfuls onto meat mixture.

Bake......... at 400° for 20 to 25 minutes until golden brown.

**For use with Pillsbury's Best Self-Rising Flour, omit baking powder and salt in biscuits.*

MAIN DISHES

For snacks, cut dough into 2½-inch rounds. Top with a scant teaspoonful of filling (you'll need only half the filling). Fold over and bake 20 to 25 minutes. Serve with sour cream.

Sunday Supper Foldovers

Senior Winner by Betty Swinger, Grand Rapids, Michigan

BAKE at 400° for 25 to 30 minutes.   MAKES 10.

Combine......	2 cups (15-oz. can) **corned beef hash** ½ cup well-drained **whole kernel corn** ⅓ cup finely chopped **green pepper** ¼ cup finely chopped **onion** 1 tablespoon prepared **mustard** and ¼ teaspoon **pepper**. Set aside.
Sift together...	2 cups sifted **Pillsbury's Best All Purpose Flour*** and 1 teaspoon **salt** into mixing bowl.
Cut in........	⅔ cup **shortening** and ⅓ cup (3-oz. pkg.) **chive cream cheese** until particles are the size of small peas.
Sprinkle......	5 to 6 tablespoons cold **water** over mixture while stirring with fork, until dough is moist enough to hold together.
Roll out.......	half at a time on floured surface to ⅛-inch thickness. Cut into 5-inch circles with a 1-pound coffee can cover; place on ungreased cookie sheet.
Place.........	¼ cup filling in rounded "V" form on center of each pastry round, keeping filling ½ inch from edge.
Shape........	by folding sides to meet over filling, making top narrower. Fasten with toothpick.
Bake.........	at 400° for 25 to 30 minutes. Serve hot with Dill Sauce.

*For use with Pillsbury's Best Self-Rising Flour, omit salt.

Dill Sauce

Combine 1 can (10½ oz.) condensed cream of celery soup, ⅔ cup milk, 1 to 2 teaspoons dill seed and ⅛ teaspoon pepper. Simmer 5 minutes. If desired, stir in 1 cup shredded Cheddar cheese.

MAIN DISHES | PAGE 11

A teen age party food. Make the dessert Angel Squares, page 26.

Beef Burger Bar-B-Que

Junior Winner by Karen Curtis, Winslow, Indiana

BAKE at 375° for 15 to 20 minutes.　　　SERVES 6 to 8.
(Makes 12x8-inch casserole.)

Soften........　1 packet **Red Star Special Active Dry Yeast** (or 1 cake Red Star Compressed Yeast) in
¼ cup warm **water** in mixing bowl.

Strain........　½ cup **condensed onion soup** (reserve remainder of 10½-oz. can).

Add..........　2 tablespoons **sugar**
2 tablespoons **shortening**, melted
½ teaspoon **salt***
1 unbeaten **egg** and strained soup to softened yeast.

Gradually add..　2 to 2¼ cups **Pillsbury's Best All Purpose Flour*** to form a soft dough, beating well. (For first additions of flour, use mixer.) Cover.

Let rise.......　in warm place (85° to 90° F.) until light and doubled in size, 45 to 60 minutes.

Hamburger Filling

Brown........　2 pounds **ground beef** in large skillet. Drain off excess fat.

Add..........　5 **frankfurters**, cut into ¼-inch diagonal slices
1 can **condensed onion soup** and reserved soup
1 cup **catsup**
½ cup **water**
1 teaspoon prepared **mustard**
¼ teaspoon **pepper** and
¼ teaspoon **chili powder**. Simmer uncovered while dough rises. Turn into 12x8-inch baking dish.

Stir..........　down dough. Drop by tablespoonfuls onto meat mixture. Sprinkle with **celery seed**.

Let rise.......　in warm place until light, about 15 minutes.

Bake.........　at 375° for 15 to 20 minutes until deep golden brown.

*For use with Pillsbury's Best Self-Rising Flour, omit salt.

MAIN DISHES

If you don't have a 3-quart casserole, two 1½-quart casseroles may be used. Make twelve 7-inch pancakes and use only half the amount of filling between each pancake. For a more Italian flavor substitute ½ lb. Italian sausage for ½ lb. ground beef.

Italian Pancake Casserole

Senior Winner by Mrs. Anthony Vulinec, Hudson, Ohio

BAKE at 375° for 30 to 35 minutes.
SERVES 8 to 10.
(Makes 3-qt. casserole.)

Sift together... into mixing bowl
- 1½ cups sifted **Pillsbury's Best All Purpose Flour***
- 1 teaspoon double-acting **baking powder**
- 1 teaspoon **salt**
- ½ teaspoon **marjoram** and
- ¼ teaspoon **garlic salt**.

Add...........
- 1 tablespoon **instant minced onion**
- ½ teaspoon **oregano** and
- ½ teaspoon **sweet basil**.

Combine......
- 2 slightly beaten **eggs** and
- 1 cup **milk**. Add to dry ingredients; mix until smooth.

Heat.......... well-greased skillet over medium high heat. Pour batter, ⅓ cup at a time, into skillet. Tilt pan and spread batter to make a 10-inch round, thin pancake. Brown about 1 minute, turn and brown on other side.

Shred........ 1 pound **Mozzarella cheese** (4 cups).

Place......... one pancake in 3-quart casserole. Spread with ¼ cup **Ricotta or creamed cottage cheese** (use 15-oz. carton in all) and 1 scant cup hot Hamburger-Tomato Sauce. Then sprinkle with ¾ cup of cheese and 1 tablespoon grated **Parmesan cheese**. Repeat layers until all pancakes and fillings are used.

Bake......... at 375° for 30 to 35 minutes until hot. Let stand about 15 minutes before serving.

**For use with Pillsbury's Best Self-Rising Flour, omit baking powder and salt.*

Hamburger-Tomato Sauce

Brown 1½ pounds ground beef with 1 small onion, chopped, in large skillet; drain off fat. Stir in 1½ cups (12-oz. can) tomato paste, 2 cups (1-lb. can) tomatoes, 1 cup water, 1 tablespoon sugar, 1 clove garlic, minced, 2 teaspoons salt, 1 teaspoon oregano, 1 teaspoon sweet basil and ½ teaspoon pepper. Cover; simmer 30 to 45 minutes, stirring occasionally.

MAIN DISHES | PAGE 13

For the Lenten season, substitute tuna or salmon for chicken. If croquettes are made early and frozen solid, let stand at room temperature about ½ hour before cutting.

Chicken Curry Croquettes

Senior Winner by Mrs. Edward L. Mirkin, Westbury, Long Island, New York

FRY at 365° F. for 4 to 5 minutes.   MAKES 16.

Melt.......... ¼ cup **Land O'Lakes Butter** in saucepan over low heat.
Stir in........ ½ cup **Pillsbury's Best All Purpose Flour**. Gradually add 1 cup **milk**. Cook, stirring constantly, until thick.
Add.......... 2 cups ground or finely chopped cooked **chicken**
¼ cup chopped **celery**
2 tablespoons chopped **parsley**
2 tablespoons **lemon juice**
1 teaspoon **salt**
1 teaspoon **celery seed**
1 teaspoon grated **onion**
1 teaspoon **gravy extract**
¼ teaspoon **curry powder**
⅛ teaspoon **pepper** and
⅛ teaspoon **hot pepper sauce**.
Stir in........ 2 unbeaten **eggs**. Heat thoroughly, stirring constantly. Spread in 8 or 9-inch piepan, lined with foil. Freeze 1½ to 2 hours until partially frozen.
Cut.......... into 16 wedges. Dip into Batter. Drain off excess Batter. Fry in deep hot fat (365° F.) for 4 to 5 minutes, turning once, until golden brown. Drain on absorbent paper. Serve with hot Chicken Sauce.

Crispy Batter

Beat.......... 2 **egg yolks** with
⅔ cup **milk** and
½ teaspoon **salt*** in large mixing bowl until well blended.
Stir in........ 1 cup **Pillsbury's Best All Purpose Flour**.*
Blend in...... 2 tablespoons **Land O'Lakes Butter**, melted
2 tablespoons **lemon juice** and
¼ teaspoon **curry powder**.
Beat.......... 2 **egg whites** until soft peaks form. Fold into batter.

*For use with Pillsbury's Best Self-Rising Flour, omit salt in Batter.

Chicken Sauce

Combine in saucepan 1 can (10½ oz.) condensed cream of chicken soup, ½ cup milk, ¼ cup drained mushroom stems and pieces, 1 teaspoon grated onion and ⅛ teaspoon curry powder. Heat thoroughly.

MAIN DISHES

Pennsylvania Knockbockle

Large shrimp, cut in pieces, may be substituted for tiny shrimp. Casserole may be served over hot cooked rice or in patty shells (see Crispy Onion Snacks, page 81).

Sea King Dinner

Sea King Dinner

Senior Winner by Mrs. Lawrence Zacker, San Diego, California

BAKE at 350° for 30 to 35 minutes.   SERVES 6 to 8.
                                         (Makes 2-qt. casserole.)

Melt......... ½ cup **Land O'Lakes Butter** in 2-quart saucepan.
Add.......... ½ cup chopped **green pepper**
              ½ cup chopped **onion** and
              ½ cup chopped **celery**. Sauté until tender.
Stir in....... ⅔ cup **Pillsbury's Best All Purpose Flour***
              ½ teaspoon **garlic salt**
              ½ teaspoon **salt**
              ¼ teaspoon **paprika** and
              ¹⁄₁₆ teaspoon **cayenne pepper**.
Add.......... 2 cups **milk**. Cook, stirring constantly, until thick. Stir in
              1 can (10 oz.) frozen **cream of shrimp soup**. Reheat.
Combine...... in 2-quart casserole
              1 can (7¾ oz.) **crab meat**, drained and boned
              1 can (4½ oz.) tiny **shrimp**, drained
              1 can (5 oz.) **water chestnuts**, drained and sliced
              1 can (4 oz.) **mushroom stems and pieces**, undrained,
              and white sauce mixture.
Combine...... 2 tablespoons **Land O'Lakes Butter**, melted
              ½ cup shredded **Cheddar cheese** and
              ½ cup **bread crumbs**. Sprinkle over casserole.
Bake......... at 350° for 30 to 35 minutes until golden brown.

*Pillsbury's Best Self-Rising Flour may be substituted.

Pennsylvania Knockbockle

Junior Winner by Caren Miller, Philadelphia, Pennsylvania

BAKE at 425° for 15 to 20 minutes.   SERVES 4 to 6.
                                         (MAKE 2-qt. casserole.)

Sauté........ in large skillet
              1 large **green pepper**, cut in strips
              2 large **onions**, sliced, and
              ½ cup (4-oz. can) drained **mushroom stems and pieces** in
              2 tablespoons **Land O'Lakes Butter** until tender.
Add.......... 2 medium **potatoes**, pared and thinly sliced
              1 teaspoon **salt** and
              1 cup **water**. Cover. Simmer 15 minutes.
Add.......... 2 cans (8 oz. each) **spaghetti sauce with mushrooms** and
              1 pound **frankfurters**, cut in ¼-inch diagonal slices.
              Cover; continue cooking until potatoes are tender.
              Turn into 2-quart casserole.

MAIN DISHES | PAGE 15

Hot Cheese Pups

Add 2 tablespoons chopped green olives or crumbled crisp bacon to cheese. Or, cut 4 frankfurters lengthwise into 4 pieces. Place on dough. Top with cheese.

Parmesan Biscuits

Sift together... 1½ cups sifted **Pillsbury's Best All Purpose Flour***
    2 teaspoons double-acting **baking powder**
    1 teaspoon **celery seed**
    ½ teaspoon **salt**

Cut in......... ¼ cup **shortening** and
    ¼ cup grated **Parmesan cheese** until particles are fine.

Combine...... 1 unbeaten **egg** with
    ⅓ cup **milk**. Add to dry ingredients; stir until dough clings together. Knead on floured surface 10 times.

Roll out....... to ½-inch thickness. Cut into rounds with floured 2-inch cutter; place on casserole.

Sprinkle...... biscuits with grated **Parmesan cheese** and **celery seed**.

Bake.......... at 425° for 15 to 20 minutes until golden brown.

**For use with Pillsbury's Best Self-Rising Flour, omit baking powder and salt in Biscuits.*

Hot Cheese Pups

Junior Winner by Elisabeth Antisdale, Oakland, California

FRY at medium heat about 8 minutes.   MAKES 16.

Soften........ 1 packet **Red Star Special Active Dry Yeast** (or 1 cake Red Star Compressed Yeast) in
    ¼ cup warm **water**.

Combine...... in mixing bowl
    1 cup hot scalded **milk**
    ¼ cup **Land O'Lakes Butter**
    2 tablespoons **sugar** and
    1½ teaspoons **salt**.* Cool to lukewarm.

Blend in...... 1 unbeaten **egg** and the softened yeast.

Gradually add.. 3½ to 4 cups **Pillsbury's Best All Purpose Flour*** to form a stiff dough; beat well after each addition. Cover.

Let rise....... in warm place (85° to 90° F.) until light and doubled in size, about 1 hour.

Combine...... 1 pound (4 cups) shredded **Cheddar cheese** and
    2 tablespoons finely chopped **onion**.

Roll out....... half of dough on floured surface to a 14x8-inch rectangle. Cut into 7x2-inch pieces. Place about 3 rounded tablespoonfuls cheese mixture down center of each strip. Bring edges to center; pinch to seal. Seal ends. Place, seam-side down, on ungreased cookie sheet. Repeat with remaining dough.

Let rise....... in warm place 30 minutes.

Fry........... in heavily-buttered skillet on medium heat (325° to 350° F.) about 2 minutes on each side. Turn carefully to brown all sides. Add butter as needed. Serve hot.

**For use with Pillsbury's Best Self-Rising Flour, omit salt.*

MAIN DISHES

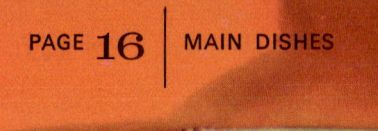

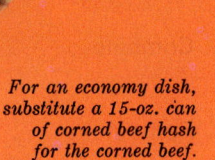

For an economy dish, substitute a 15-oz. can of corned beef hash for the corned beef.

Corned Beef Wheels

Senior Winner by Mrs. Jack C. Jones, Long Beach, California

BAKE at 425° for 25 to 30 minutes. MAKES 12.

Sauté . . . . ½ cup finely chopped **onion** and
½ cup (4-oz. can) drained **mushroom stems and pieces** in
3 tablespoons **Land O'Lakes Butter**. Reserve ¼ cup.

Stir in . . . . ⅓ cup dairy **sour cream**
⅓ cup **tomato soup** (reserve remainder of 10½-oz. can)
1 can (12 oz.) **corned beef**, finely chopped
1 tablespoon **Worcestershire sauce** and
⅛ teaspoon hot **pepper sauce**. Chill while preparing dough.

Caraway Biscuits

Sift together . . . into mixing bowl
2 cups sifted **Pillsbury's Best All Purpose Flour***
3 teaspoons double-acting **baking powder**
1 teaspoon dry **mustard**
½ teaspoon **salt**

Cut in . . . . ½ cup **Land O'Lakes Butter** until particles are fine.

Add . . . . 1 unbeaten **egg**
2 teaspoons **caraway seed** and
¼ cup **milk**. Stir until dough clings together.

Roll out . . . . on floured waxed paper to a 14x12-inch rectangle. Spread with filling. Roll up, starting with 14-inch side; seal edge. Cut into 12 slices. Place in greased 12x8-inch baking dish.

Bake . . . . at 425° for 25 to 30 minutes. Serve hot with Sauce.

*For use with Pillsbury's Best Self-Rising Flour, omit baking powder and salt.

Sour Cream-Tomato Sauce

Combine 1 cup dairy sour cream, remainder of tomato soup, ½ teaspoon salt, ⅛ teaspoon pepper and reserved onion-mushroom mixture in top of double boiler. Heat thoroughly over boiling water. If too thick, thin with milk.

Just right for a buffet supper. Basic ingredients should be measured accurately. Seasonings may be varied to suit family tastes.

Chicken Delish

Senior Winner by Mrs. Lawrence McKinin, Columbia, Missouri

BAKE at 375° for 45 to 50 minutes.   SERVES 6 to 8.
(Makes 12x8-inch casserole.)

Sift together... 2 cups sifted **Pillsbury's Best All Purpose Flour***
3 teaspoons double-acting **baking powder** and
½ teaspoon **salt** into mixing bowl.

Cut in........ ½ cup **Land O'Lakes Butter** until particles are fine.

Combine...... 1 unbeaten **egg** with
½ cup **milk**. Add to dry ingredients; stir until dough is formed. Divide into 2 parts, one slightly larger.

Roll out....... larger piece on floured surface to a 15x12-inch rectangle. Fit into an ungreased 12x8-inch baking dish, pressing dough against sides and bottom of dish.

Chicken Filling

Combine...... 3 cups cooked, diced **chicken**
1 cup cooked, diced **ham**
1 cup (8-oz. can) drained **mushroom stems and pieces**
½ cup **Pillsbury's Best All Purpose Flour** and
½ cup toasted, sliced **almonds.** Turn into pastry-lined pan.

Roll out....... remaining dough to a 12x7-inch rectangle. Cut lengthwise into 1-inch strips. Place 4 strips lengthwise over filling. Cut remaining strips in half and place crosswise over filling making a lattice top.

Combine...... 2 cups hot **chicken broth**
1 cup light **cream**
1 teaspoon **salt**
¼ to ½ teaspoon **nutmeg**
⅛ to ¼ teaspoon **allspice** and
⅛ teaspoon **pepper.** Pour over lattice top.

Bake......... at 375° for 45 to 50 minutes until golden brown.

**For use with Pillsbury's Best Self-Rising Flour, omit baking powder and salt in crust.*

MAIN DISHES

Extra biscuits may be baked in a small pan for 15 to 20 minutes or until golden brown.

Sweet Cherry Ham Bake

Senior Winner by Mrs. Mary C. Endicott, Atlanta, Georgia

BAKE at 425° for 25 to 30 minutes. SERVES 6 to 8.
(Makes 12x8-inch casserole.)

Combine...... 4 cups (1 lb.) ground smoked **ham**
1 cup finely chopped **celery**
⅓ cup **milk**
½ teaspoon dry **mustard** and
1 unbeaten **egg**. Spread in 12x8-inch baking dish.

Drain........ 1 can (1 lb.) **sour pie cherries**; reserve juice.
Combine...... in saucepan
¼ cup **sugar**
¼ cup firmly packed **brown sugar** and
2 tablespoons **corn starch**. Add
¼ teaspoon **Burnett's Red Food Coloring**
½ cup **water** and reserved cherry juice. Cook, stirring constantly, until thickened. Reserve ½ cup for topping.

Add......... 3 tablespoons **lemon juice** and cherries to remainder. Spoon over ham.

Parkerhouse Biscuits

Sift together... into mixing bowl
2½ cups sifted **Pillsbury's Best All Purpose Flour***
1 tablespoon **sugar**
4 teaspoons double-acting **baking powder** and
1 teaspoon **salt**.

Cut in........ ⅓ cup **shortening** until particles are fine.
Combine...... ¾ cup **milk** and
1 unbeaten **egg**. Add to dry ingredients; mix until dry particles are moistened. Knead on floured surface 12 strokes.

Roll out....... to ¼-inch thickness. Cut into rounds with floured 2½-inch cutter. Mark a crease with dull edge of knife to one side of center of each round. Place small pat of **Land O'Lakes Butter** on larger part. Fold small part over butter; press to seal. Place on cherry-meat mixture.

Bake......... at 425° for 25 to 30 minutes until golden brown. Pour reserved sauce over biscuits.

**For use with Pillsbury's Best Self-Rising Flour, omit baking powder and salt.*

MAIN DISHES | PAGE 19

To save last minute time, bake rolls early in the day. To reheat, wrap in foil and place in a 350° oven for 10 to 15 minutes. For Friday, substitute 2 cans (6½ oz. each) tuna for the meat. Omit broiling.

Hidden Cheeseburgers

Senior Winner by Mrs. Paul T. Bartlett, Tulsa, Oklahoma

BAKE at 375° for 15 to 20 minutes.   MAKES 1 dozen.

Soften......... 1 packet **Red Star Special Active Dry Yeast** (or 1 cake Red Star Compressed Yeast) in
1 cup warm **water** in mixing bowl.

Add.......... 3 tablespoons **sugar**
3 tablespoons **shortening**, melted
1½ teaspoons **salt*** and
1 unbeaten **egg**.

Gradually add.. 3¼ to 3½ cups **Pillsbury's Best All Purpose Flour*** to form a stiff dough, beating well. Cover. Chill at least 2 hours. Prepare Hamburgers.

Roll out....... dough on floured surface to a 16x15-inch rectangle. Cut into 4x5-inch strips. Place Hamburger on each strip. Bring dough around Hamburger; seal edges. Place, seam-side down, on ungreased cookie sheets.

Combine...... ¼ cup dairy **sour cream**
¼ teaspoon **salt**
⅛ teaspoon **white pepper** and
⅛ teaspoon **garlic salt**. Spread on top of rolls. Cover.

Let rise....... in warm place until light, about 45 minutes.

Bake......... at 375° for 15 to 20 minutes until brown. Serve hot.

Hamburgers

Combine...... ½ cup shredded **Cheddar cheese**
2 tablespoons soft **Land O'Lakes Butter**
2 tablespoons finely chopped **onion** and
2 teaspoons prepared **mustard**; mix well. Set aside.

Combine...... 1½ pounds **ground beef**
1 can (4½ oz.) **deviled ham**, if desired
1 unbeaten **egg**
1½ teaspoons **salt** and
¼ teaspoon **pepper**; mix well. Divide into 12 equal parts.

Shape........ into oblongs, 4 inches long. Make deep cut down center; fill with a rounded teaspoonful cheese filling; seal edges. Broil or fry until well browned; drain well.

*For use with Pillsbury's Best Self-Rising Flour, omit salt in dough.

PAGE 20 | CAKES

Umejiro F. Kuritsubo, an Oakland, California gardener was one of only two men in the 15th Bake-Off. He came to bake his one and only recipe—the only one he needed to win the $1,000 Best of Class Cake award.

To cut angel food or sponge cakes, use a serrated knife. Place end of knife in center of cake, then cut at an angle with a gentle sawing motion.

Walnut Glory Cake

Senior Best of Class Winner by Mr. Umejiro Frank Kuritsubo, Oakland, California

BAKE at 350° for 55 to 65 minutes.   MAKES 10-inch tube cake.

Combine...... ¾ cup **Pillsbury's Best All Purpose Flour***
2 teaspoons **cinnamon**
1 teaspoon **salt**

Beat......... 9 **egg whites** (1¼ cups) in large mixing bowl until soft mounds form. Gradually add
¾ cup **sugar.** Continue beating until very stiff, straight peaks form. **Do not underbeat.**

Combine...... 9 **egg yolks**
2 teaspoons **Burnett's Pure Vanilla** and
¾ cup **sugar** in small mixing bowl. Beat until thick and lemon colored. Stir in dry ingredients.

Fold......... batter gently but thoroughly into egg whites using a wire whip or rubber spatula. Fold in
2 cups finely chopped **Diamond Walnuts.**

Turn......... into ungreased 10-inch tube pan.

Bake......... at 350° for 55 to 65 minutes. **Invert immediately.** Cool completely before removing from pan. Frost with a vanilla glaze, sprinkle with confectioners' sugar or serve with whipped cream.

*For use with Pillsbury's Best Self-Rising Flour, omit salt.

CAKES

Rocky Road Nut Cake

Senior Winner by Mrs. W. Stuart Smith, San Antonio, Texas

BAKE at 350° for 35 to 40 minutes.   MAKES 13x9-inch cake.

Sift together....	into mixing bowl 1½ cups sifted **Pillsbury's Best All Purpose Flour*** 1¾ cups **sugar** ½ teaspoon **salt**
Add.........	4 unbeaten **eggs** and 1 teaspoon **Burnett's Pure Vanilla**; beat well.
Stir in.......	1½ cups chopped **Diamond Walnuts**.
Fold in......	1 cup **Land O'Lakes Butter**, melted; mix well.
Turn.........	into 13x9-inch pan, greased and floured on bottom.
Bake.........	at 350° for 35 to 40 minutes until cake springs back when touched in center. Sprinkle immediately with 4 cups **miniature marshmallows**. Drizzle with Icing.

*Self-rising flour is not recommended for use in this recipe.

Butterscotch Icing

Combine in small saucepan 1 cup firmly packed brown sugar, ⅓ cup milk, ¼ cup Land O'Lakes Butter and ¼ teaspoon salt. Bring to a boil; boil 3 minutes. Add 1 cup sifted confectioners' sugar; beat well.

Tropical Orange Cake

Senior Winner by Mrs. Huey Hilburn, Piedmont, Alabama

BAKE at 350° for 25 to 30 minutes.   MAKES 13x9-inch cake.

Cream........	½ cup **Land O'Lakes Butter**. Gradually add 1 cup **sugar**, creaming well.
Blend in......	2 unbeaten **eggs**, one at a time, beating well after each.
Combine......	1 teaspoon **soda*** and ¾ cup **buttermilk** or sour milk.
Add..........	1½ cups sifted **Pillsbury's Best All Purpose Flour*** alternately with buttermilk to butter mixture.
Coat.........	1 cup finely cut **dates** 1 cup finely cut **candied orange pieces** and 1 cup chopped **Diamond Walnuts** with ¼ cup **flour**. Fold into batter.
Turn.........	into 13x9-inch pan, greased and floured on bottom.
Bake.........	at 350° for 25 to 30 minutes until cake springs back when touched lightly in center. Cool and frost.

*For use with Pillsbury's Best Self-Rising Flour, decrease soda to ½ teaspoon.

Orange Coconut Frosting

Cream ¼ cup Land O'Lakes Butter. Gradually add 2 cups sifted confectioners' sugar, creaming well. Blend in 2 tablespoons orange juice and ½ cup flaked or chopped shredded coconut.

CAKES | PAGE 23

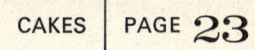

Rocky Road Nut Cake—
For cupcakes, fill muffin cups, lined with paper baking cups, half full. Bake 20 to 25 minutes. Top with 2 cups miniature marshmallows. If glaze thickens, thin with a few drops milk. Makes 24.

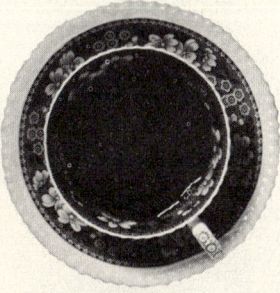

Tropical Orange Cake—
Cool rectangular loaf cakes in pan on wire rack. Frost cake in pan. If your pan doesn't have a cover, make one from foil or slip cake into a large plastic bag.

Sweet Applets—
Serve as a cake or serve warm as a muffin. Sweet Applets may be wrapped in foil and heated in a 350° oven for 10 to 15 minutes.

Sweet Applets

Senior Winner by Mrs. Louise Kidd, Artesia, New Mexico

BAKE at 400° for 20 to 25 minutes.   MAKES 12.

Sift together... 1½ cups sifted **Pillsbury's Best All Purpose Flour***
2 teaspoons double-acting **baking powder**
½ teaspoon **salt** and
½ teaspoon **nutmeg.** Set aside.

Add.......... ½ cup **sugar** gradually to
⅓ cup **shortening,** creaming well.

Blend in...... 1 unbeaten **egg**; mix well.

Add.......... ⅓ cup **milk** alternately with dry ingredients.

Stir in........1½ cups pared, shredded **apple.**

Fill........... well-greased muffin cups two-thirds full.

Bake......... at 400° for 20 to 25 minutes until golden brown. Remove from pan; cool 10 minutes. Dip in
¼ cup **Land O'Lakes Butter,** melted, then roll in mixture of
½ cup **sugar** and
1 teaspoon **cinnamon.** Serve warm or cold.

*For use with Pillsbury's Best Self-Rising Flour, omit baking powder and salt.

Place pans in oven so they do not touch each other or sides of oven. If your oven will not accommodate 3 layers or you don't have 3 pans hold the extra batter in refrigerator. Bake as soon as oven or pan is available.

Chocolate Celebration Cake

Senior Winner by Mrs. Laverne Buckley, Collins, New York

BAKE at 350° for 30 to 35 minutes. MAKES three 8-inch layers.

Sift together...	into mixing bowl
	2¼ cups sifted **Pillsbury's Best All Purpose Flour***
	1 package (4 oz.) **chocolate pudding and pie filling mix**
	1 teaspoon **salt**
	1 teaspoon **soda**
Add..........	1½ cups firmly packed **brown sugar**
	⅔ cup **shortening** and
	1 cup **buttermilk** or sour milk.
Beat.........	1½ minutes. (With electric mixer, blend at lowest speed, then beat at a low speed. Or beat 225 strokes with a spoon.)
Add..........	3 unbeaten **eggs** and
	1 teaspoon **Burnett's Pure Vanilla**. Beat 1½ minutes.
Turn.........	into three 8-inch round layer pans, greased and floured on bottoms. (Use about 1½ cups batter per pan.)
Sprinkle......	1 cup (6-oz. pkg.) **Nestlé's Semi-Sweet Chocolate Morsels** over layers.
Bake.........	at 350° for 30 to 35 minutes until cake springs back when touched lightly in center. Cool. Frost, stacking layers top-side up. Decorate with **Diamond Walnuts**.

*For use with Pillsbury's Best Self-Rising Flour, omit salt and soda.

Chocolate Frosting

Melt 1 cup (6-oz. pkg.) Nestlé's Semi-Sweet Chocolate Morsels and ¼ cup Land O'Lakes Butter in ⅓ cup milk in saucepan over low heat. Remove from heat. Stir in 1 pound (4 to 4½ cups) sifted confectioners' sugar. If necessary, thin with a few drops of milk.

Cake may be baked in two 9x5x3-inch pans.

Kentucky Butter Cake

Senior Winner by Mrs. Albert G. Lewis, Jr., Platte City, Missouri

BAKE at 325° for 60 to 65 minutes.   MAKES 10-inch tube cake.

Sift together...	3 cups sifted **Pillsbury's Best All Purpose Flour*** 1 teaspoon double-acting **baking powder** 1 teaspoon **salt** ½ teaspoon **soda**
Cream........	1 cup **Land O'Lakes Butter.** Gradually add 2 cups **sugar,** creaming well.
Blend in......	4 unbeaten **eggs,** one at a time, beating well after each.
Combine......	1 cup **buttermilk** or sour milk and 2 teaspoons **Burnett's Pure Vanilla.** Add alternately with the dry ingredients to creamed mixture, beginning and ending with dry ingredients. Blend well after each addition. (With electric mixer, use low speed.)
Turn.........	into 10-inch tube pan, greased on the bottom.
Bake.........	at 325° for 60 to 65 minutes until cake springs back when touched in center. Run spatula along edge and stem of pan. Prick cake with fork. Pour hot Sauce over cake. Cool before removing from pan. Just before serving, sprinkle with confectioners' sugar.

*For use with Pillsbury's Best Self-Rising Flour, omit baking powder, salt and soda.

Butter Sauce

Combine in saucepan 1 cup sugar, ¼ cup water and ½ cup Land O'Lakes Butter. Heat until butter is melted; do not boil. Add 1 tablespoon Burnett's Pure Vanilla or Burnett's Rum Flavor.

Quick trick. Leave cake in pan and frost top only. You'll need only half the frosting recipe and half of the cashews.

Angel Squares

Senior Winner by Mrs. Alvin D. Albertus, Cedar Rapids, Iowa

BAKE at 350° for 35 to 40 minutes.   MAKES 13x9-inch cake.

Sift together...   into mixing bowl
2 cups sifted **Pillsbury's Best All Purpose Flour***
2 cups **sugar**
2 teaspoons double-acting **baking powder**
1 teaspoon **salt**

Blend in...... 1 cup hot **milk** and
1 teaspoon **Burnett's Pure Vanilla.** Beat 2 minutes. (With mixer, blend at lowest speed, then beat at medium speed. Or beat 300 strokes with a spoon.)

Beat......... 7 **egg whites** (1 cup) and
½ teaspoon **cream of tartar** in large mixing bowl until soft peaks form. Fold into batter, gently but thoroughly.

Turn......... into 13x9-inch pan, greased and floured on bottom.

Bake......... at 350° for 35 to 40 minutes until cake springs back when touched lightly in center. Cool. Cut into 3x2-inch rectangles. Frost top and sides. Roll in 1½ to 2 cups **cashew nuts** or salted peanuts, finely chopped. Drizzle with Chocolate Glaze.

*For use with Pillsbury's Best Self-Rising Flour, omit baking powder and salt.

Butter Frosting

Combine ¼ cup soft Land O'Lakes Butter, 1 pound (4 to 4½ cups) sifted confectioners' sugar and 1 teaspoon Burnett's Pure Vanilla. Blend in 5 to 6 tablespoons milk until of spreading consistency.

Chocolate Glaze

Melt 2 five-cent Nestlé's Milk Chocolate Candy Bars, 2 tablespoons milk and 1 tablespoon Land O'Lakes Butter over hot water.

CAKES | PAGE **27**

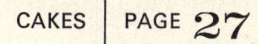

How to measure Land O'Lakes Butter:
4 sticks (1 lb.) = 2 cups
2 sticks (½ lb.) = 1 cup
1 stick (¼ lb.) = ½ cup or 8 tablespoons
½ stick (⅛ lb.) = ¼ cup or 4 tablespoons

Lemon Butter Layers

Senior Winner by Mrs. Jack Albanese, Great Falls, Montana

BAKE at 325° for 55 to 60 minutes.   MAKES 9 or 10-inch tube cake.

Sift together...   2 cups sifted **Pillsbury's Best All Purpose Flour***
                 2¼ teaspoons double-acting **baking powder**
                 ½ teaspoon **salt**

Cream.......   1 cup **Land O'Lakes Butter** with
                 1 teaspoon **Burnett's Lemon Extract.** Gradually add
                 1¼ cups **sugar**, creaming well, 5 to 8 minutes. (The more you beat, the better the cake.)

Blend in......   6 unbeaten **eggs**, one at a time; beat 1 minute after each.

Add.........   the dry ingredients; blend thoroughly.

Turn........   into 9 or 10-inch tube pan, greased on the bottom.

Bake........   at 325° for 55 to 60 minutes until cake springs back when touched lightly in center. **Do not invert.** Cool.

Cut.........   cake horizontally to make 4 layers. Stack layers, spreading Filling and sprinkling 2 tablespoons Nut Crunch on each layer and on top.

**For use with Pillsbury's Best Self-Rising Flour, omit baking powder and salt.*

Lemon Cream Filling

Prepare 1 package (3½ to 4 oz.) lemon pudding and pie filling mix using ⅔ cup sugar and 2 cups water. Cool to lukewarm. Cream ¾ cup Land O'Lakes Butter. Gradually add filling, beating well. Cool thoroughly.

Nut Crunch

Heat ½ cup sugar in small skillet until sugar melts and is golden brown. Stir in ¾ cup chopped Diamond Walnuts or almonds. Spread on greased cookie sheet; cool. Crush fine. (To crush nut mixture, place between sheets of waxed paper and crush with hammer or rolling pin.)

CAKES

- If you don't have a 15x10x1-inch pan, make one from heavy foil. Place on a cookie sheet.
- Just right as an after school snack with a glass of milk.

Cinnamon Toast Cake

Junior Winner by John Anderson, Cooperstown, New York

BAKE at 350° for 20 to 25 minutes, then for 10 minutes.   MAKES 15x10-inch cake.

Sift together...   into mixing bowl
2 cups sifted **Pillsbury's Best All Purpose Flour***
1 cup **sugar**
2 teaspoons double-acting **baking powder**
1 teaspoon **salt**

Blend in......   1 cup **milk**
2 tablespoons **Land O'Lakes Butter**, melted
1 teaspoon **Burnett's Pure Vanilla** and
½ cup **raisins**, if desired. Mix well.

Turn.........   into 15x10x1-inch jelly roll pan, well greased and lightly floured on the bottom.

Bake.........   at 350° for 20 to 25 minutes until golden brown.

Drizzle.......   ½ cup **Land O'Lakes Butter**, melted, over cake. Combine
½ cup **sugar** and
1½ teaspoons **cinnamon**. Sprinkle over cake.

Bake.........   at 350° for 10 minutes.

*For use with Pillsbury's Best Self-Rising Flour, omit baking powder and salt.

CAKES | PAGE **29**

When using glass ovenware or dull-finished metal decrease the oven temperature 25° as these pans absorb heat readily and brown cakes more quickly.

Upside Down Penuche Cake

Senior Winner by Mrs. Helen Pope, Arroyo Grande, California

BAKE at 350° for 30 to 35 minutes.*   MAKES 13x9-inch cake.

Melt......... ¼ cup **Land O'Lakes Butter** in 13x9-inch pan. Stir in
         1 cup firmly packed **brown sugar**
         ¼ cup light **cream**
         ¾ cup sliced **pecans** and
         1⅓ cups (3½-oz. can) flaked **coconut**.

Beat......... 3 **egg whites** in small bowl until foamy. Gradually add ¼ cup **sugar**. Continue beating until stiff peaks form.

Sift together... into large mixing bowl
         2 cups sifted **Pillsbury's Best All Purpose Flour***
         1 cup **sugar**
         3 teaspoons double-acting **baking powder**
         ½ teaspoon **salt**

Add.......... ½ cup soft **Land O'Lakes Butter** and
         1 cup light **cream**.

Beat......... 1½ minutes. (With electric mixer, blend at lowest speed, then beat at a low speed. Or beat 225 strokes with a spoon.)

Add.......... 3 **egg yolks** and
         1 teaspoon **Burnett's Pure Vanilla**. Beat 1½ minutes.

Fold in....... egg whites. Spoon over mixture in pan.

Bake......... at 350° for 30 to 35 minutes until cake springs back when touched lightly in center. Cool 2 minutes; loosen edges and turn out onto wire rack or serving plate.

*For use with Pillsbury's Best Self-Rising Flour, omit baking powder and salt. Increase baking time to 35 to 40 minutes.

CAKES

To sour milk, combine 2 tablespoons vinegar with enough milk to measure 1 cup.

Plantation Pride Cake

Senior Winner by Mrs. Dwight E. Maples, Wildwood, Florida

BAKE at 375° for 25 to 30 minutes.   MAKES 13x9-inch cake.

Sift together...	2 cups sifted **Pillsbury's Best All Purpose Flour*** 1 tablespoon **cocoa** 1 teaspoon **soda** ½ teaspoon **salt**
Melt.........	½ cup **Land O'Lakes Butter** with 1 cup **buttermilk** or sour milk. Cool to room temperature.
Combine......	1¾ cups firmly packed **brown sugar** 2 unbeaten **eggs** and 1 teaspoon **Burnett's Pure Vanilla** in mixing bowl.
Add.........	dry ingredients alternately with buttermilk mixture, beginning and ending with dry ingredients. (With electric mixer, use a low speed.)
Turn.........	into 13x9-inch pan, greased and floured on bottom.
Bake.........	at 375° for 25 to 30 minutes until cake springs back when touched lightly in center. Spread with Topping.
Broil.........	watching carefully until bubbly and golden brown, 2 to 3 minutes.

*For use with Pillsbury's Best Self-Rising Flour, omit soda and salt.

Topping

Melt ½ cup **Land O'Lakes Butter** in saucepan. Add 1 cup firmly packed **brown sugar**; heat until sugar dissolves. Add 1 cup flaked **coconut**, ½ cup chopped **Diamond Walnuts**, ¼ cup **evaporated milk** or cream and 1 tablespoon **Burnett's Pure Vanilla**.

Cake may be baked in two 9x5x3-inch pans lined with foil and well greased on bottom. Bake at 350° for 40 to 45 minutes.

Butterscotch Sundae Treat

Senior Winner by Mrs. Guy H. Little, Hickory, North Carolina

BAKE at 350° for 60 to 65 minutes.　　　　　MAKES 10-inch cake.

Drain.........	1 can (8¾ oz.) crushed **pineapple**; reserve ¼ cup juice.
Melt..........	1 cup (6-oz. pkg.) **Nestlé's Butterscotch Morsels** over hot water. Blend in
	¼ cup soft **Land O'Lakes Butter** and reserved pineapple juice. Set aside ¼ cup.
Spread.......	pineapple in bottom of 10-inch (8 cup) gugelhupf pan, well greased on bottom. Pour butterscotch mixture over pineapple. Spread sides with mixture of
	¼ cup soft **Land O'Lakes Butter**
	¼ cup chopped **Diamond Walnuts**
	3 tablespoons **brown sugar** and
	10 cut **maraschino cherries**.
Sift together...	2 cups sifted **Pillsbury's Best All Purpose Flour***
	1 teaspoon **soda**
	1 teaspoon **salt**
Cream.........	½ cup **Land O'Lakes Butter** or shortening. Gradually add
	1¼ cups **sugar**, creaming well.
Blend in......	3 unbeaten **eggs,** one at a time, beating well after each, and reserved butterscotch mixture.
Add..........	the dry ingredients alternately with
	¾ cup **buttermilk** or sour milk, beginning and ending with dry ingredients. (With mixer, use a low speed.)
Stir in........	½ cup chopped **Diamond Walnuts.**
Turn..........	into prepared pan.
Bake..........	at 350° for 60 to 65 minutes. Cool 2 minutes; remove from pan. Drizzle with Vanilla Glaze.

*For use with Pillsbury's Best Self-Rising Flour, omit soda and salt.

Vanilla Glaze

Combine 1 cup sifted confectioners' sugar, 1½ to 2 tablespoons milk and ½ teaspoon **Burnett's Pure Vanilla.**

PAGE **32** | CAKES

Store cakes with custard, cream or whipped cream fillings in refrigerator. Keep covered so they won't pick up flavors.

Jamaican Mystery Cake

Senior Winner by Mrs. Louis Fedrizzi, Detroit, Michigan

BAKE at 350° for 30 to 35 minutes. MAKES two 8-inch layers.

Sift together...	into mixing bowl 2¼ cups sifted **Pillsbury's Best All Purpose Flour*** 1⅓ cups **sugar** 3 teaspoons double-acting **baking powder** 1 teaspoon **salt**
Add.........	1 cup **milk** and ½ cup **shortening**.
Beat........	1½ minutes. (With electric mixer, blend at lowest speed, then beat at a low speed. Or beat 225 strokes with a spoon.)
Add.........	2 unbeaten **eggs** and 1½ teaspoons **Burnett's Pure Vanilla**. Beat 1½ minutes.
Turn........	into two 8-inch round layer pans, well greased and lightly floured on the bottoms.
Bake........	at 350° for 30 to 35 minutes. Cool. Prick each layer several times with a fork.
Combine.....	in small saucepan ½ cup **sugar** 1½ tablespoons **Nescafé Instant Coffee** and ½ cup **water**. Bring to a boil; boil 4 minutes. Spoon over cake layers. Cool. Fill and frost.

*For use with Pillsbury's Best Self-Rising Flour, omit baking powder and salt.

Rum Cream Filling

Combine ⅓ cup flour, ⅓ cup sugar and ¼ teaspoon salt in saucepan. Gradually add 1½ cups milk and 3 beaten egg yolks (or 2 eggs). Cook, stirring constantly, until thick. Stir in 2 tablespoons Land O'Lakes Butter and 2 teaspoons Burnett's Rum Flavor. Cover; chill. Reserve ½ cup for Frosting.

Whipped Cream Frosting

Beat 1 cup whipping cream with ¼ cup confectioners' sugar and the reserved Cream Filling until thick.

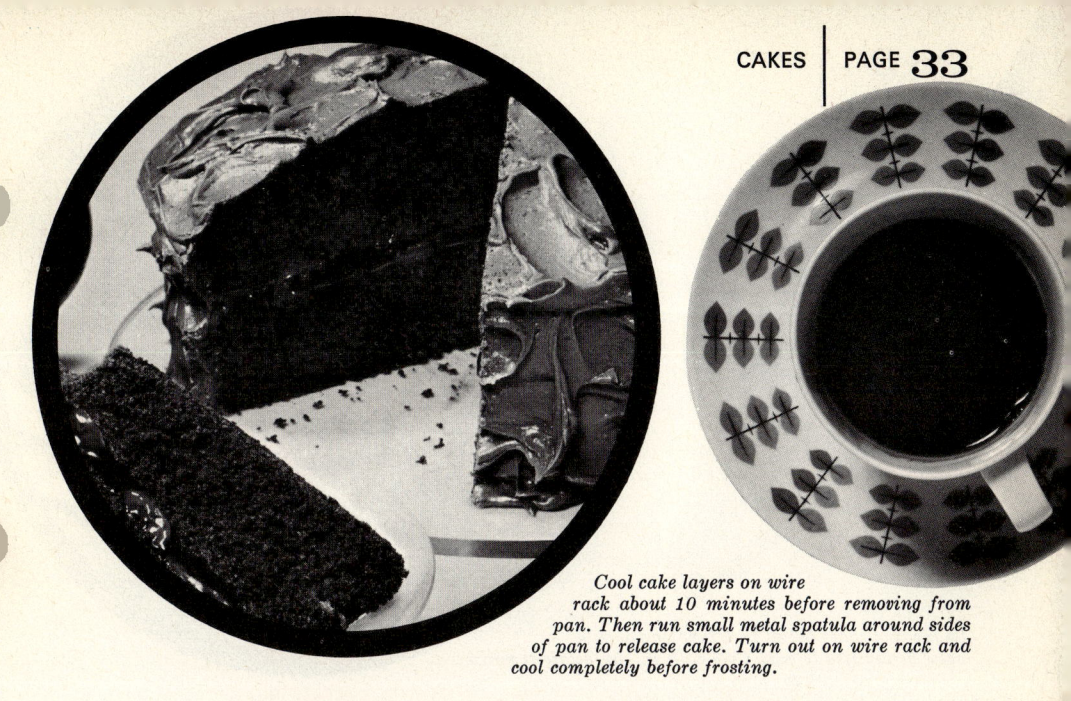

Cool cake layers on wire rack about 10 minutes before removing from pan. Then run small metal spatula around sides of pan to release cake. Turn out on wire rack and cool completely before frosting.

Cherry Almond Fudge Cake

Senior Winner by Mrs. Gerald E. Ames, Gorham, Maine

BAKE at 350° for 35 to 40 minutes.　　　MAKES two 9-inch layers.

Combine......　　3 squares (3 oz.) unsweetened **chocolate**
　　　　　　　　½ cup **milk** and
　　　　　　　　½ cup **sugar** in saucepan. Cook, stirring constantly, until thick and smooth. Stir in
　　　　　　　　1 teaspoon **Burnett's Almond Extract** and
　　　　　　　　1 cup **cherry pie filling** (reserve remainder of 1 lb. 5-oz. can for filling). Cool.

Sift together...　2 cups sifted **Pillsbury's Best All Purpose Flour***
　　　　　　　　1 teaspoon **soda** and
　　　　　　　　1 teaspoon **salt.** Set aside.

Add..........　　1 cup **sugar** gradually to
　　　　　　　　½ cup **shortening,** creaming well.

Blend in......　　3 unbeaten **eggs,** one at a time, beating well after each.

Add..........　　the dry ingredients alternately with
　　　　　　　　¾ cup **milk,** beginning and ending with dry ingredients. Blend well after each addition. Stir in chocolate.

Turn.........　　into two 9-inch round layer pans, well greased and lightly floured on the bottoms.

Bake.........　　at 350° for 35 to 40 minutes until cake springs back when touched lightly in center. Cool. Spread reserved cherry filling between layers. Frost top and sides.

*Self-rising flour is not recommended for use in this recipe.

Chocolate Cream Cheese Frosting

Soften ⅓ cup (3-oz. pkg.) cream cheese with 3 tablespoons milk and ¼ teaspoon salt. Gradually add 1 pound (4 to 4½ cups) sifted confectioners' sugar; blend thoroughly. Add 1½ squares (1½ oz.) melted unsweetened chocolate and ½ teaspoon Burnett's Almond Extract. Beat until smooth. If necessary, thin with more milk.

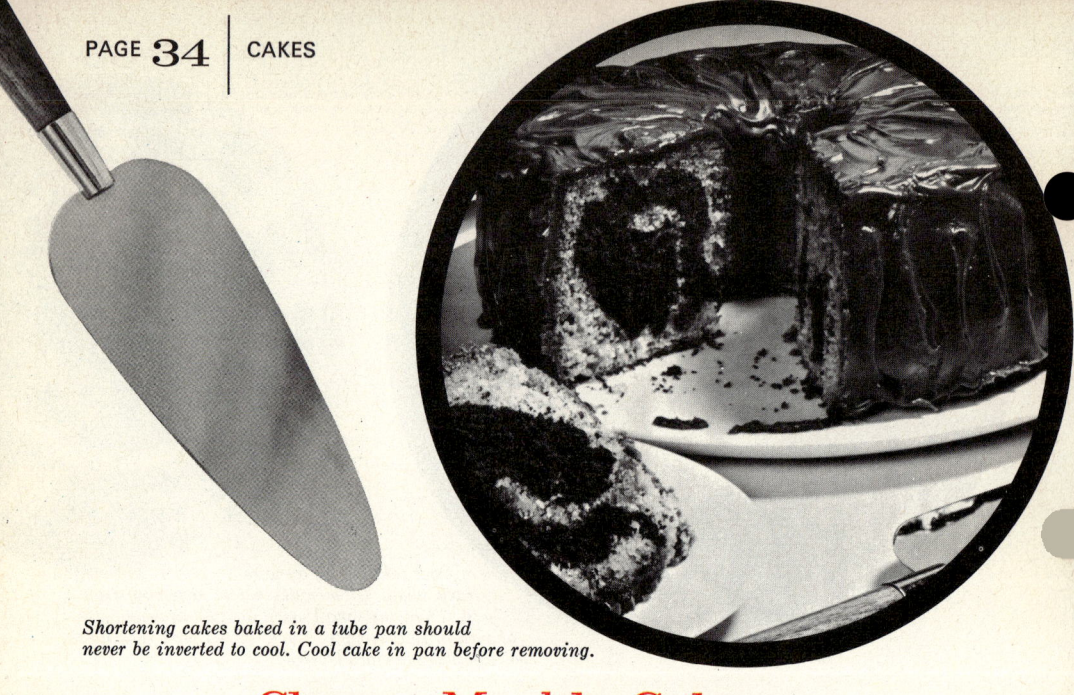

PAGE 34   CAKES

Shortening cakes baked in a tube pan should never be inverted to cool. Cool cake in pan before removing.

Cherry Marble Cake

Senior Winner by Mrs. Morris Hansburg, Youngstown, Ohio

BAKE at 350° for 60 to 65 minutes.   MAKES 9 or 10-inch tube cake.

Sift together...	2½ cups sifted **Pillsbury's Best All Purpose Flour***
	1½ teaspoons **soda**
	½ teaspoon **salt**
Cream.........	¾ cup **Land O'Lakes Butter**. Gradually add
	1¼ cups **sugar**, creaming well.
Blend in......	2 unbeaten **eggs**; beat well.
Combine......	1 cup dairy **sour cream**
	¼ cup **maraschino cherry juice** and
	¼ cup **water**. Add alternately with dry ingredients to creamed mixture, beginning and ending with dry ingredients. Blend well after each addition. (With electric mixer, use a low speed.)
Place.........	4 cups of batter in a bowl. Stir in
	½ cup chopped **Diamond Walnuts** and
	½ cup finely cut **maraschino cherries**.
Blend........	2 squares (2 oz.) melted unsweetened **chocolate** into remaining batter.
Spoon........	cherry and chocolate batter alternately into 9 or 10-inch tube pan, well greased on bottom.
Bake.........	at 350° for 60 to 65 minutes until cake springs back when touched lightly. **Do not invert**. Cool and frost.

*Self-rising flour is not recommended for use in this recipe.

Fudge Frosting

Combine in saucepan 2 squares (2 oz.) unsweetened chocolate (or 1 cup Nestlé's Semi-Sweet Chocolate Morsels), 1 cup sugar, ¼ cup Land O'Lakes Butter, ⅓ cup milk and ¼ teaspoon salt. Bring to a boil; simmer 3 minutes. Remove from heat. Blend in 2 cups sifted confectioners' sugar and 1 teaspoon Burnett's Pure Vanilla; beat well. Thin with milk while frosting cake.

CAKES | PAGE 35

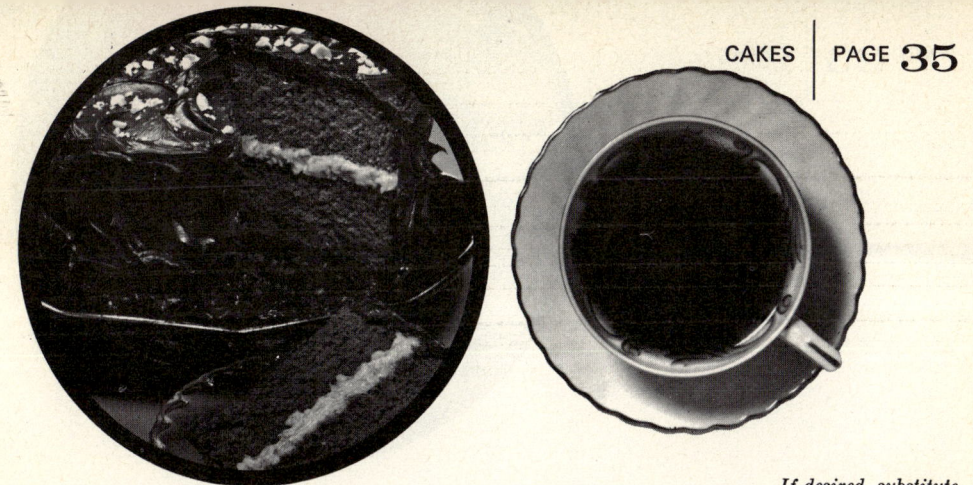

If desired, substitute 1 cup (6-oz. pkg.) Nestlé's Semi-Sweet Chocolate Morsels for the sweet cooking chocolate in cake and ½ cup chocolate morsels for unsweetened chocolate in Frosting.

Brown Velvet Cake

Senior Winner by Mrs. V. H. Shermer, Klamath Falls, Oregon

BAKE at 350° for 35 to 40 minutes.　　　MAKES two 9-inch layers.

Combine......　1 bar (¼ lb.) **sweet cooking chocolate** and
　　　　　　　½ cup **boiling water**. Let stand; stir to combine.

Sift together...　2½ cups sifted **Pillsbury's Best All Purpose Flour***
　　　　　　　1 teaspoon **soda**
　　　　　　　½ teaspoon **salt**

Cream.........　½ cup **Land O'Lakes Butter** with
　　　　　　　½ cup **peanut butter**. Gradually add
　　　　　　　1 cup firmly packed **brown sugar** and
　　　　　　　½ cup **sugar**, creaming well.

Add..........　2 unbeaten **eggs**
　　　　　　　2 **egg whites** (reserve yolks for Filling)
　　　　　　　1 teaspoon **Burnett's Pure Vanilla** and the chocolate.

Add..........　the dry ingredients alternately with
　　　　　　　1 cup **buttermilk** or sour milk, beginning and ending with dry ingredients. Blend well after each addition.

Turn.........　into two 9-inch round layer pans, well greased and lightly floured on the bottoms.

Bake.........　at 350° for 35 to 40 minutes. Cool; fill and frost. Sprinkle with reserved nuts.

**For use with Pillsbury's Best Self-Rising Flour, decrease soda to ¼ teaspoon and omit salt.*

Creamy Peanut Filling

Combine in saucepan ½ cup firmly packed brown sugar and 1 tablespoon corn starch. Add ½ cup evaporated milk, ¼ cup water and 2 egg yolks. Cook over medium heat, stirring constantly, until thick. Remove from heat. Stir in ½ cup chopped peanuts (reserve 2 tablespoons), 1 tablespoon peanut butter and ½ teaspoon Burnett's Pure Vanilla. Cool.

Brown Velvet Frosting

Cream 2 tablespoons Land O'Lakes Butter and 2 tablespoons peanut butter. Add 1½ squares (1½ oz.) melted unsweetened chocolate and 1 teaspoon Burnett's Pure Vanilla. Blend in 3 cups sifted confectioners' sugar alternately with 4 to 5 tablespoons milk until of spreading consistency.

CAKES

Store layer cakes under "cake server" with roomy cover that fits over plate or tray. Or, invert a large bowl over the plate.

Imperial Crown Cake

Senior Winner by Mrs. J. G. Gullett, Duluth, Georgia

BAKE at 375° for 25 to 30 minutes.   MAKES two 9-inch layers.

Melt.......... ⅔ cup **Nestlé's Semi-Sweet Chocolate Morsels** and
⅓ cup **Nestlé's Butterscotch Morsels** in
¼ cup **water** in saucepan over low heat. Cool.

Sift together... 2¼ cups sifted **Pillsbury's Best All Purpose Flour***
1 teaspoon **salt** and
1 teaspoon **soda**. Set aside.

Add.......... 1¼ cups **sugar** gradually to
½ cup **shortening**, creaming well.

Blend in...... 3 unbeaten **eggs**, one at a time; beat well. Stir in
1 teaspoon **Burnett's Pure Vanilla** and chocolate mixture.

Add.......... the dry ingredients alternately with
1 cup **buttermilk** or sour milk, beginning and ending with dry ingredients. Blend well after each addition.

Turn.......... into two 9-inch round layer pans, well greased and lightly floured on the bottoms.

Bake.......... at 375° for 25 to 30 minutes. Cool. Spread Frosting between layers and on sides. Spread top with Topping.

*For use with Pillsbury's Best Self-Rising Flour, omit salt and soda.

Sea Foam Frosting

Combine in top of double boiler ⅓ cup firmly packed brown sugar, ⅓ cup sugar, ¼ cup corn syrup, 2 egg whites, 2 tablespoons water, ¼ teaspoon salt and ¼ teaspoon cream of tartar. Cook over boiling water, beating constantly with electric mixer or rotary beater until mixture stands in peaks. Remove from heat. Add ½ teaspoon Burnett's Pure Vanilla and ½ teaspoon Burnett's Maple Flavor, if desired; continue beating until frosting holds deep swirls. Reserve 1 cup for Topping.

Chocolate Tuft Topping

Sauté ½ cup coarsely chopped pecans in 1 tablespoon Land O'Lakes Butter until golden brown. Drain on absorbent paper. Melt ⅓ cup Nestlé's Semi-Sweet Chocolate Morsels and ¼ cup Nestlé's Butterscotch Morsels. Cool. Combine pecans, chocolate mixture and reserved Frosting.

To cut a frosted layer cake, use a long thin, sharp knife rinsed in hot water. Cut through with a gentle sawing motion; don't press down. Rinse knife after each cut.

Peanut Butter and Jelly Cake

Senior Winner by Mrs. Ruth Hill Molloy, Fort Eustis, Virginia

BAKE at 375° for 30 to 35 minutes.   MAKES two 9-inch layers.

Sift together...   into mixing bowl
                       2½ cups sifted **Pillsbury's Best All Purpose Flour***
                       ⅔ cup **sugar**
                       4 teaspoons double-acting **baking powder**
                       ½ teaspoon **salt**

Add.........   1 cup firmly packed **brown sugar**
                       ⅓ cup **shortening**
                       ⅓ cup **peanut butter** and
                       1¼ cups **milk**.

Beat.........   1½ minutes. (With electric mixer, blend at lowest speed, then beat at a low speed. Or beat 225 strokes with a spoon.)

Add.........   3 unbeaten **eggs** and
                       1 teaspoon **Burnett's Pure Vanilla**. Beat 1½ minutes.

Turn.........   into two 9-inch round layer pans, well greased and lightly floured on the bottoms.

Bake.........   at 375° for 30 to 35 minutes until cake springs back when touched lightly in center. Cool. Place one layer, top-side down, on serving plate. Spread with
                       ¼ cup **peanut butter** then with
                       ½ cup **red jelly**. Top with second layer; frost.

*For use with Pillsbury's Best Self-Rising Flour, omit baking powder and salt.

Fluffy Frosting

Combine in top of double boiler ¾ cup sugar, ¼ cup light corn syrup, 2 tablespoons water, 2 unbeaten egg whites, ¼ teaspoon salt and ¼ teaspoon cream of tartar. Cook over rapidly boiling water, beating with electric mixer or rotary beater until mixture stands in peaks. Remove from heat. Add 1 teaspoon Burnett's Pure Vanilla; beat until frosting holds deep swirls.

Ice Cream Cake

Senior Winner by Mrs. Perna Mae Ramsey, Oklahoma City, Oklahoma

BAKE at 375° for 25 to 30 minutes.   MAKES two 9-inch layers.

Combine......	1 package (3¼ oz.) **vanilla pudding and pie filling mix**
	1 teaspoon **Nescafé Instant Coffee** and
	1 cup **milk** in saucepan. Cook over medium heat, stirring constantly, until slightly thickened.
Add.........	1 cup (½ pt.) **vanilla ice cream** and
	¼ cup **Nestlé's Butterscotch Morsels**. Continue cooking until thick. Remove from heat; cool.
Sift together...	2¼ cups sifted **Pillsbury Best All Purpose Flour***
	4 teaspoons double-acting **baking powder**
	1 teaspoon **salt** and
	1 teaspoon **cinnamon**. Set aside.
Add.........	1 cup **sugar** gradually to
	⅔ cup **shortening**, creaming well.
Blend in.....	3 unbeaten **eggs**, one at a time, beating well after each.
Add.........	dry ingredients alternately with butterscotch mixture, beginning and ending with dry ingredients. Blend well after each addition. (With mixer, use a low speed.)
Turn.........	into two 9-inch round layer pans, well greased and lightly floured on bottoms.
Bake.........	at 375° for 25 to 30 minutes until cake springs back when touched lightly in center. Cool. Fill and frost.

*For use with Pillsbury's Best Self-Rising Flour, omit baking powder and salt.

Butterscotch Coconut Frosting

Combine in saucepan ½ cup Land O'Lakes Butter, ¼ cup strong coffee and ¼ cup Nestlé's Butterscotch Morsels. Cook over low heat until morsels melt. Blend in 1 pound (4 to 4½ cups) sifted confectioners' sugar and ¼ teaspoon cinnamon. Beat until smooth and of spreading consistency. Stir in ½ cup flaked coconut. If necessary, thin with a few drops milk.

Old Time Chocolate Cake

Senior Winner by Mrs. William Snodgrass, Hanna City, Illinois

BAKE at 350° for 30 to 35 minutes.   MAKES two 8-inch layers.

Sift together...	1½ cups sifted **Pillsbury's Best All Purpose Flour***
	⅓ cup **instant nonfat dry milk**
	1 teaspoon **soda**
	½ teaspoon **salt**
Melt.........	1 cup (6-oz. pkg.) **Nestlé's Semi-Sweet Chocolate Morsels** and
	½ cup **Land O'Lakes Butter** with
	1 cup **water** in top of double boiler over hot water. Remove from heat.
Add.........	1 cup quick-cooking **rolled oats**
	1 cup **sugar** and
	½ cup **water**. Mix thoroughly.
Beat in......	2 unbeaten **eggs**
	1 teaspoon **Burnett's Pure Vanilla** and
	¼ teaspoon **Burnett's Red Food Coloring**.

CAKES | PAGE 39

Ice Cream Cake—Frosting should hold deep swirls when spread on cake. If it thickens while standing, thin with a few drops of milk.

Old Time Chocolate Cake—Cake may be baked in a 13x9-inch pan.

Gradually add..	dry ingredients, mixing well after each addition.
Stir in........	1 cup packaged grated **coconut** or chopped **Diamond Walnuts**. Turn into two 8-inch round layer pans, well greased and lightly floured on the bottoms.
Bake.........	at 350° for 30 to 35 minutes. Cool and frost.

*For use with Pillsbury's Best Self-Rising Flour, omit soda and salt.

Honey Chocolate Frosting

Melt 1 cup (6-oz. pkg.) Nestlé's Semi-Sweet Chocolate Morsels and 2 tablespoons Land O'Lakes Butter with 2 tablespoons milk in top of double boiler over hot water. Remove from heat. Blend in ¼ cup honey, 1 teaspoon Burnett's Pure Vanilla, ¼ teaspoon Burnett's Red Food Coloring and ⅛ teaspoon salt. Gradually add 2 cups sifted confectioners' sugar; beat until of spreading consistency. If necessary, thin with a few drops of milk.

PAGE 40 | COOKIES

Mrs. Charles Mallinson of Kansas City, Missouri, didn't come to the Bake-Off to bake. Instead she came with a no-bake fudge cookie inspired by her two youngsters' confusion of cookies and fudge candy. It won the $1,000 Best of Class Cookie prize.

For a richer chocolate flavor, increase morsels to 2 cups, or add ¼ cup cocoa to the evaporated milk mixture before cooking.

COOKIES | PAGE 41

Fudge Nougats

Senior Best of Class Winner by Mrs. Dagmar Mallinson, Kansas City, Missouri

MAKES 40 pieces.

Combine...... in saucepan
 2 cups **sugar**
 ½ cup **Land O'Lakes Butter** and
 1 cup **evaporated milk.** Bring to a full rolling boil, stirring constantly. Boil 10 minutes, stirring occasionally.

Stir in........ 1 cup (6-oz. pkg.) **Nestlé's Semi-Sweet Chocolate Morsels**
 ¾ cup **Pillsbury's Best All Purpose Flour***
 1 cup finely crushed **graham crackers**
 ¾ cup chopped **Diamond Walnuts** and
 1 teaspoon **Burnett's Pure Vanilla.**

Spread....... in well-buttered 12x8 or 9x9-inch pan. If desired, top with Diamond Walnut Halves, one for each piece. Cool. (For faster setting, place candy in refrigerator.) Cut into squares.

*Pillsbury's Best Self-Rising Flour may be substituted.

Refrigerator cookie doughs are handy to have on hand and bake fresh for unexpected company. If well wrapped the dough will stay fresh 2 to 3 weeks.

Butter Crunch Slices

Senior Winner by Mrs. Frank McCue, Portland, Oregon

BAKE at 350° for 12 to 15 minutes.   MAKES about 6 dozen cookies.

Combine......	1 cup (6-oz. pkg.) **Nestlé's Butterscotch Morsels**, melted ⅓ cup **sweetened condensed milk** ¼ cup **peanut butter** 1 tablespoon **Land O'Lakes Butter** 1 cup salted **peanuts**, finely chopped, and 1 teaspoon **Burnett's Pure Vanilla**. Chill; prepare cookies.
Cream........	½ cup **Land O'Lakes Butter** and ¼ cup **peanut butter** with ½ cup **granulated or confectioners' sugar** and ½ teaspoon **salt**.*
Add..........	1 cup sifted **Pillsbury's Best All Purpose Flour*** and ½ cup quick-cooking **rolled oats**; mix to form a dough.
Divide........	dough in half. Roll out each to a 12x6-inch rectangle on floured waxed paper. Shape filling into two 12-inch rolls on rectangles. Roll dough around filling. Wrap; chill at least 2 hours.
Cut..........	into ¼-inch slices. Place on ungreased cookie sheets.
Bake.........	at 350° for 12 to 15 minutes until lightly browned. Cool slightly before removing from cookie sheet.

For use with Pillsbury's Best Self-Rising Flour, omit salt.

For a flavor variation in Oriental Treasure Cookies, add ¼ cup whole wheat flour to dry ingredients. Decrease all purpose flour to 1½ cups.

Oriental Treasure Cookies

Senior Winner by Mrs. John R. Stegmuller, Lahina, Maui, Hawaii

BAKE at 350° for 12 to 15 minutes.   MAKES about 3 dozen.

Sift together...	1⅔ cups sifted **Pillsbury's Best All Purpose Flour*** 1½ teaspoons double-acting **baking powder** and ½ teaspoon **soda**. Set aside.
Gradually add..	½ cup firmly packed **brown sugar** and ½ cup **sugar** to ½ cup **shortening**, creaming well.
Blend in......	1 unbeaten **egg** 1 tablespoon **soy sauce** and ½ teaspoon **Burnett's Almond Extract**; beat well.
Add..........	the dry ingredients gradually; mix thoroughly.
Combine......	½ cup slivered **almonds** with 1 teaspoon **sugar** and ½ teaspoon **soy sauce**.
Shape........	dough into balls; use rounded teaspoonful for each. Dip tops in almonds. Place on ungreased cookie sheets.
Bake.........	at 350° for 12 to 15 minutes until golden brown.

For use with Pillsbury's Best Self-Rising Flour, omit baking powder and soda.

COOKIES | PAGE 43

Macaroon Polka Dots

Senior Winner by Mrs. Lois Vouga, St. Louis, Missouri

BAKE at 325° for 15 minutes, then for 25 to 30 minutes.*   MAKES about 3 dozen bars.

Cream........	⅓ cup **Land O'Lakes Butter**. Add ½ cup firmly packed **brown sugar**; cream well.
Add.........	2 **egg yolks** 1 teaspoon **Burnett's Pure Vanilla** ¼ teaspoon **soda*** and ¼ teaspoon **salt**; beat well.
Blend in......	1 cup **Pillsbury's Best All Purpose Flour;*** mix thoroughly.
Spread.......	in 11x7 or 9x9-inch pan, greased on the bottom.
Bake.........	at 325° for 15 minutes.* Do not brown.
Beat.........	2 **egg whites** until soft peaks form. Add 1 tablespoon **sugar**; continue beating until stiff peaks form.
Fold in.......	¾ cup **sweetened condensed milk** ½ cup **Nestlé's Semi-Sweet Chocolate Morsels** and 2 cups packaged grated **coconut**. Spread over base.
Bake.........	at 325° for 25 to 30 minutes until light golden brown. Cool; cut into bars.

For use with Pillsbury's Best Self-Rising Flour, omit soda and salt. Bake base 20 minutes.

Apple Harvest Squares may be cut in 2-inch squares and served as a cookie. Or, cut into 4-inch squares and top with ice cream for a dessert. Serve warm or cold.

Apple Harvest Squares

Senior Winner by Mrs. Rex Pippin, Sr., Dothan, Alabama

BAKE at 375° for 20 minutes, then for 25 to 30 minutes.   MAKES 2 dozen.

Sift together...	1½ cups sifted **Pillsbury's Best All Purpose Flour*** ⅓ cup **sugar** and ¾ teaspoon **salt** into mixing bowl.
Cut in........	½ cup **Land O'Lakes Butter** until particles are fine. Press into bottom of 13x9-inch pan.
Arrange......	4 cups pared, sliced **apples** (about 4 medium) over base.
Sprinkle with..	2 tablespoons **lemon juice**.
Combine......	⅓ cup **sugar** and 1 teaspoon **cinnamon**; sprinkle over apples.
Bake.........	at 375° for 20 minutes.
Combine......	½ cup **sugar** 1 unbeaten **egg** ⅓ cup **evaporated milk** 1 teaspoon **Burnett's Pure Vanilla** ¾ cup chopped **Diamond Walnuts** and 1⅓ cups (3½-oz. can) flaked **coconut**. Spoon over apples.
Bake.........	at 375° for 25 to 30 minutes until golden brown.

For use with Pillsbury's Best Self-Rising Flour, omit salt.

COOKIES

Simple trick. Flatten cookies with a glass which has a design on bottom.

Frosted Fruit Jumbles
Senior Winner by Mrs. Jean C. Wehler, Hyattsville, Maryland

BAKE at 375° for 9 to 12 minutes.   MAKES about 7 dozen cookies.

Sift together...	4 cups sifted **Pillsbury's Best All Purpose Flour***
	1 teaspoon **salt**
	1 teaspoon **soda**
	½ teaspoon **mace**
	½ teaspoon **nutmeg**
Add.........	2 cups mixed **candied fruit**
	½ cup **raisins** and
	½ cup chopped **Diamond Walnuts**; mix well.
Cream.......	1 cup **Land O'Lakes Butter**. Gradually add
	¾ cup firmly packed **brown sugar** and
	½ cup **sugar,** creaming well.
Blend in.....	2 unbeaten **eggs**
	1 teaspoon **Burnett's Pure Vanilla** and
	1 teaspoon **Burnett's Lemon Extract**; beat well. Add half the flour-fruit mixture; mix well.
Add.........	⅓ cup dairy **sour cream**. Blend in remaining flour mixture. Chill at least 2 hours.
Shape.......	dough into balls, using a rounded teaspoonful for each. Place on ungreased cookie sheets. Flatten to ¼-inch thickness with bottom of glass dipped in sugar.
Bake........	at 375° for 9 to 12 minutes until light golden brown. Frost warm with Lemon Glaze.

*For use with Pillsbury's Best Self-Rising Flour, omit salt and soda.

Lemon Glaze
Combine 2 tablespoons Land O'Lakes Butter, 2 cups sifted confectioners' sugar and 1 teaspoon Burnett's Lemon Extract. Add 2 to 3 tablespoons milk until of spreading consistency.

Crunchy Date Slices may be shaped into balls, then rolled in peanut crunch mixture.

Crunchy Date Slices
Junior Winner by Nancy Ellen Ferchak, Jessup, Pennsylvania

BAKE at 400° for 12 to 15 minutes.   MAKES about 2½ dozen cookies.

Cream.......	½ cup **Land O'Lakes Butter** with
	⅓ cup firmly packed **brown sugar**.
Add.........	1 cup **Pillsbury's Best All Purpose Flour.*** Mix until a dough will form. Stir in
	½ cup **peanuts,** chopped. Crumble onto a cookie sheet.
Bake........	at 400° for 12 to 15 minutes until golden brown. Cool.
Combine.....	in saucepan
	1 cup cut **dates**
	½ cup **Nestlé's Semi-Sweet Chocolate Morsels** and
	¼ cup **water**. Cook over medium heat until thick; cool.
Stir in.......	2¼ cups peanut crunch mixture, broken in small pieces. Crush remaining crunch mixture.
Shape.......	chocolate-date mixture into two 8-inch rolls. Roll in peanut crunch mixture. Wrap; store in refrigerator. To serve, cut into ¼-inch slices.

*Pillsbury's Best Self-Rising Flour may be substituted.

COOKIES | PAGE 45

Spicicles

Senior Winner by Mrs. N. Mergel, Glenshaw, Pennsylvania

BAKE at 350° for 10 to 15 minutes.   MAKES 5 to 6 dozen cookies.

Sift together... 2½ cups sifted **Pillsbury's Best All Purpose Flour***
 ½ teaspoon **salt**
 ¼ teaspoon **cinnamon**
 ¼ teaspoon **cloves**
 ¼ teaspoon **cardamom**

Grind....... 1 cup **raisins** with
 ½ cup **dates**
 1 slice **candied pineapple** or ¼ cup candied cherries and
 ¾ cup **Diamond Walnuts**. Add to dry ingredients. Mix until fruits and nuts are coated with dry ingredients.

Cream....... 1 cup **Land O'Lakes Butter**. Gradually add
 1 cup sifted **confectioners' sugar**, creaming well.

Blend in...... 1 unbeaten **egg**; beat well.

Add......... dry ingredients; blend well. Chill at least 2 hours.

Shape....... tablespoonfuls of dough into ½-inch rolls on lightly floured surface. Cut into 4-inch pieces. Place on ungreased cookie sheets.

Bake........ at 350° for 10 to 15 minutes until light golden brown. Cool. Frost and dip in packaged grated **coconut** or roll warm unfrosted cookies in **confectioners' sugar**.

*For use with Pillsbury's Best Self-Rising Flour, omit salt.

Spicy Butter Frosting

Combine 2 tablespoons soft Land O'Lakes Butter, 2 cups sifted confectioners' sugar, ¼ teaspoon cardamom, ⅛ teaspoon cinnamon, 2 tablespoons milk and ½ teaspoon Burnett's Pure Vanilla.

Long Ago Lemon Cookies

Senior Winner by Mrs. Mathilde T. Bass, Berlin, New Hampshire

BAKE at 375° for 10 to 15 minutes.   MAKES 3 to 4 dozen.

Sift together... 2¼ cups sifted **Pillsbury's Best All Purpose Flour***
 ¾ teaspoon **salt**

Combine...... in mixing bowl
 2 cups dairy **sour cream**
 1⅓ cups **sugar**
 1 teaspoon **soda** and
 1½ teaspoons grated **lemon rind** or **Burnett's Lemon Extract**.

Stir in....... ¼ cup **Land O'Lakes Butter**, melted, and dry ingredients.

Drop........ by heaping teaspoonfuls onto greased cookie sheets.

Sprinkle..... with mixture of
 ¼ cup **sugar** and
 ¼ teaspoon **mace** or nutmeg.

Bake........ at 375° for 10 to 15 minutes until very lightly browned.

*For use with Pillsbury's Best Self-Rising Flour, decrease soda to ¼ teaspoon and omit salt.

COOKIES

Tip: A 15x10x1-inch pan may be made from heavy foil.

Butterscotch Pinwheels
Junior Winner by Scherry Ann Pesante, Roswell, New Mexico

BAKE at 325° for 8 minutes.   MAKES about 5 dozen cookies.

Melt .... 1 cup (6-oz. pkg.) **Nestlé's Semi-Sweet Chocolate Morsels** and
2 tablespoons **shortening** in top of double boiler over boiling water. Remove from heat.

Add .... 1 can (15 oz.) **sweetened condensed milk**
1 cup **Pillsbury's Best All Purpose Flour*** and
1 teaspoon **Burnett's Pure Vanilla**. Blend well.

Spread ...... in 15x10x1-inch jelly roll pan which has been greased, lined with waxed paper and greased again.

Bake .... at 325° for 8 minutes. Prepare Filling while baking. Immediately turn chocolate base onto a towel which has been sprinkled lightly with confectioners' sugar. Spread with Filling. Sprinkle with
½ cup chopped **Diamond Walnuts**.

Roll up ...... starting with 15-inch side. Wrap; store in refrigerator. To serve, cut into ¼-inch slices.

**Pillsbury's Best Self-Rising Flour may be substituted.*

Butterscotch Filling

Melt 1 cup (6-oz. pkg.) **Nestlé's Butterscotch Morsels** with 2 tablespoons shortening in top of double boiler over boiling water.

Lemon-y Layers is another cookie that can be substituted for a dessert. Cut in 3-inch squares and serve topped with ice cream or sweetened whipped cream.

Lemon-y Layers
Senior Winner by Mrs. Marie V. Brennan, Daly City, California

BAKE at 350° for 10 minutes, then   MAKES 2 dozen bars.
for 30 to 35 minutes.

Combine ..... 1 cup sifted **Pillsbury's Best All Purpose Flour*** and
¼ cup firmly packed **brown sugar** in mixing bowl.

Cut in .... ½ cup **Land O'Lakes Butter** until particles are fine.

Press .... into greased 8-inch square pan.

Bake .... at 350° for 10 minutes. Do not brown.

Combine ..... in small saucepan
½ cup firmly packed **brown sugar**
1 tablespoon **corn starch**
¼ cup frozen **lemonade concentrate** and
⅛ teaspoon **salt**; cook until mixture thickens.

Add .... ½ cup chopped **Diamond Walnuts**. Spread over base.

Combine ..... 2 beaten **eggs**
1⅓ cups (3½-oz. can) flaked **coconut** and
1 teaspoon **Burnett's Pure Vanilla**; spoon over filling.

Bake .... at 350° for 30 to 35 minutes until golden brown. Cool; cut into bars.

**Pillsbury's Best Self-Rising Flour may be substituted.*

- For puffier cookies, use 4½ or 9-oz. milk chocolate bars, cut into rectangles, or miniature milk chocolate bars.
- For extra fancy touch, sprinkle with chopped Diamond Walnuts, colored sugars or coconut before baking.

Chocolate Pillows

Second Grand Prize Winner by Gemma Jane Hall, Olympia, Washington

BAKE at 375° for 12 to 15 minutes.   MAKES 4 to 5 dozen cookies.

Sift together... 2½ cups sifted **Pillsbury's Best All Purpose Flour***
½ teaspoon **salt**

Cream........ 1 cup **Land O'Lakes Butter**. Gradually add
¾ cup **sugar**, creaming well.

Blend in...... 1 unbeaten **egg** and
2 teaspoons **Burnett's Pure Vanilla**; beat well.

Stir in........ the dry ingredients.

Press........ dough through a cookie press, using saw-tooth (spritz) plate, into strips onto ungreased cookie sheets.

Cut.......... 10 five-cent **Nestlé's Milk Chocolate Candy Bars** into 1-inch pieces. Place ¼ inch apart on strips of dough. Press another strip of dough over candy, covering completely. Mark bars between chocolate pieces.

Bake......... at 375° for 12 to 15 minutes until light golden brown. Cut into pieces immediately.

*For use with Pillsbury's Best Self-Rising Flour, omit salt.

Chocolate Beau Catchers

Junior Winner by Merry Dee Melinsky, Howard Lake, Minnesota

BAKE at 350° for 10 to 12 minutes.   MAKES about 5 dozen cookies.

Sift together... 2 cups sifted **Pillsbury's Best All Purpose Flour***
½ teaspoon **soda**
½ teaspoon **salt**

Cream........ ¾ cup **Land O'Lakes Butter**. Gradually add
1 cup **sugar**, creaming well.

Blend in......1½ squares (1½ oz.) melted unsweetened **chocolate**
1 teaspoon **Burnett's Pure Vanilla** and
1 unbeaten **egg**; beat well.

Add.......... ½ cup **milk** alternately with the dry ingredients. Mix well.

Stir in........1¼ cups (8-oz. pkg.) cut **dates** and
½ cup chopped **Diamond Walnuts**.

Drop......... by rounded teaspoonfuls onto greased cookie sheets.

Bake......... at 350° for 10 to 12 minutes. Cool and frost.

*For use with Pillsbury's Best Self-Rising Flour, omit soda and salt.

Browned Butter Frosting

Brown ¼ cup Land O'Lakes Butter in saucepan. Blend in 2 cups sifted confectioners' sugar and 2 to 3 tablespoons water until of desired consistency.

PAGE 48 | COOKIES

Butter Crunch Slices—page 42   Oriental Treasure Cookies—page 42   Macaroon Polka Dots—page 43

Spicicles—page 45   Long Ago Lemon Cookies—page 45   Butterscotch Pinwheels—page 46

Ginger Boys—page 51   Walnut Sandwich Cookies—page 51

Candy Surprises—page 53   Chocolate Shadows—p. 54

HOW TO WIN $25,000
and a trip to Florida too!

bake-off '64

Stay in Miami Beach's luxurious Americana Hotel! Sunshine, sea, and excitement! All expenses paid!

Enter Pillsbury's Grand National Bake-Off *Now.* You could win!

You may have a winner in your recipe box right now!

Here are some hints to help you choose a recipe or recipes to enter. (Send in several. See Easy Rules for Winning.)

Choose a family favorite. One that homemakers from coast to coast would like to have in their recipe collection.

Choose one with ingredients easily available.

It should be easy to make and look good, but need not be fancy.

Bake your recipe from the entry before you send it in. Then you'll be sure you haven't left out some important ingredient or step.

READ THE RULES FOR WINNING. JUST TURN THIS PAGE.

DO IT NOW! CONTEST CLOSES MAY 31.
Entries received later will automatically be entered in next year's BAKE-OFF.

EASY RULES FOR WINNING

Contest Closes May 31.

1. On an Official Entry Blank, print or type your name and address. Check the division you are entering (one only): Junior or Senior, and the type recipe you consider yours to be. **JUNIORS:** Also state your age and date of birth in the spaces provided.

2. Print or type your recipe on a separate sheet or sheets of paper giving every ingredient and amount used in making your recipe. Print or type your name and address at the top of each sheet. Using one side of the paper only and any recipe style you desire, give the following information:
   - Measurements in level (not scant or heaping) cups, tablespoons, teaspoons, or in fractions (¼, ⅓, ½, etc.)
   - Baking time and temperature
   - Name of your recipe

   Brand names of ingredients may be given if desired but are not required.

3. Attach your recipe and an extra-value coupon or trade-mark from any size package of Pillsbury Flour firmly to the Official Entry Blank.

4. Enclose your entry in an envelope addressed to PILLSBURY'S BEST BAKE-OFF, Box 2C, Minneapolis, Minnesota 55460. Entries must be postmarked not later than **May 31** and received not later than **June 5** to be eligible for this year. Any entries received after this date will be eligible for the following year. You may send in as many entries as you wish, but only one per envelope. All recipes and entries become the property of The Pillsbury Company and cannot be acknowledged or returned.

OFFICIAL ENTRY BLANK

PILLSBURY'S $100,000 GRAND NATIONAL BAKE-OFF
Contest Closes May 31

Mail to Pillsbury's Best Bake-Off, Box 2C, Minneapolis, Minnesota 55460

Name_____
Please Print
Address_____
City_____ State_____ Zip_____

☐ **JUNIOR** (Any boy or girl 12 through 18 on March 1, this year)
AGE_____ DATE OF BIRTH_____

☐ **SENIOR** (Anyone 19 or over on March 1, this year)

CHECK TYPE OF RECIPE:
☐ Cakes ☐ Cookies ☐ Breads ☐ Main Dishes ☐ Pies ☐ Desserts

I buy my flour from Store_____
(list one store only):
Street_____
City_____ State_____

IMPORTANT:
1. Print your name and address. Give recipe on separate sheet and attach.
2. Attach to this entry blank the EXTRA-VALUE COUPON OR TRADE-MARK from any size package of Pillsbury's Best Regular or Self-Rising Flour or Pillsbury Instant Blending Flour.

SPECIAL GENERAL ELECTRIC BONUS AWARD
For Qualified Grand National Finalists—$150 Cash Wardrobe Gift

Here's how Grand National Finalists Qualify:

1. Go to any franchised General Electric dealer and have him demonstrate the official General Electric Bake-Off range to you.
2. Have him sign this official Pillsbury entry blank in the space provided below. That's all there is to it! You will be awarded $150 cash for your Bake-Off trip wardrobe.

_____
(Dealer's signature and date)

_____
(Dealer's address)

SPECIAL OFFER! If you buy a General Electric range between now and May 31, and if you are one of the 100 finalists in the Bake-Off, General Electric will give you back DOUBLE the money you paid for the range in place of the range you win as a finalist. You can't lose. (To qualify for this special award, get a receipted copy of the invoice from your dealer and mail prior to May 31st to R. W. Curtis, General Electric Company, Building 2, Room 227, Appliance Park, Louisville 1, Kentucky. Invoice must contain model and serial number.)

CONTEST CLOSES MAY 31, ENTER NOW!

5. To be considered, every entry:
  - Must comply with above rules.
  - Must call for at least one-half cup of Pillsbury Flour (not cake flour or mixes).
  - Must not call for an intoxicating beverage.
  - Must call for ingredients usually found in grocery stores.
  - Must be able to be completely prepared in one day.

6. Ten Winners will be selected from each state, Puerto Rico, District of Columbia and the U.S. Armed Forces, making a total of 530 state winners. The 100 Bake-Off finalists will be selected from these 530 state winners and will compete at the Bake-Off.

7. Everyone 12 years or over on March 1, of this year and living in the United States, or Puerto Rico and overseas members of the U.S. Armed Forces and their dependents may enter—except employees of the following organizations and members of their immediate families: The Pillsbury Co., its advertising agencies and judging organizations, employees of the General Electric Company, practicing professional home economists and professional chefs and bakers. Entrants 19 years or over on March 1, this year, are eligible for Senior Grand National Awards; entrants 12 through 18 are eligible for Junior Grand National Awards. All entrants are eligible for the two top awards of $25,000 and $5,000.

8. An international Judging Agency and a staff of home economists will judge qualified entries in the Recipe Contest on the basis of general appeal, ease and speed of preparation, and novelty or unusual character.

9. The Baking Contest will be limited to the 80 Senior Recipe Contest Finalists and the 20 Junior Recipe Contest Finalists. Entrants will prepare their prize-winning recipes without assistance. Entries will be judged on the basis of general appeal, taste, appearance and novelty. No entrant will be eligible for more than one cash award in the Baking Contest.

10. These rules are binding on all entrants. The decisions of the judges will be final. In the cases of ties, duplicate awards will be made. This contest is subject to federal and local laws. Names and addresses of all winners will be furnished after December 1, upon request.

OVER $100,000 IN PRIZES

$25,000
FIRST GRAND PRIZE

$5,000
SECOND GRAND PRIZE

$6,500
in SENIOR PRIZES

$3,000 . . . . 1st Senior Prize
$2,000 . . . . 2nd Senior Prize
$1,500 . . . . 3rd Senior Prize

$4,500
in JUNIOR PRIZES

$3,000 . . . . 1st Junior Prize
$1,000 . . . . 2nd Junior Prize
$ 500 . . . . 3rd Junior Prize

$4,000
SENIOR 'BEST OF CLASS' AWARDS

$1,000 . . . . BEST CAKE
$1,000 . . . . BEST BREAD OR MAIN DISH
$1,000 . . . . BEST COOKIES
$1,000 . . . . BEST PIE OR DESSERT
100 GE J408 Deluxe Double Oven Ranges
100 GE All-Purpose Mixers
$100 in Cash to Each of the 100 Finalists

SPECIAL 530 STATE WINNERS

10 winners will be selected from each state, Puerto Rico, District of Columbia and the U.S. Armed Forces, making a total of 530 state winners. These state winners will receive a personalized award of recognition. The 100 Grand National Finalists will be selected from these state winners and will compete at the Bake-Off.

120 ALL-EXPENSE PAID TRIPS TO MIAMI BEACH

Finalists competing in the baking contest receive an all-expense paid trip to Miami Beach, stay at the fabulous Americana Hotel and receive a cash prize of $100. 80 finalists in the Senior division and 20 finalists in the Junior division will make the trip. Each of the junior finalists may bring one parent or approved adult with all expenses paid by Pillsbury.

3 EXCLUSIVE OFFERS!

1 For your Grand National Cook Books—
A NEW DELUXE COOKBOOK BINDER
with convenient self-storing stand.
ONLY $1.25   ORDER YOURS TODAY

---

2 Special offer to 15th Grand National Bake-Off cookbook owners.
PILLSBURY'S BEST OF THE BAKE-OFF COLLECTION
A wonderful cookbook containing 1,000 prize winning recipes—100 each from the first ten Pillsbury Grand National Bake-Offs.
Standard edition (regular price $4.95) only $3.95
Deluxe edition (regular price $5.95) only $4.95
Save $1.00 over book store prices on either edition.

---

3 **THE 14TH GRAND NATIONAL BAKE-OFF COOKBOOK**
is still available to you. If you haven't obtained your copy, you can do so now.
ONLY 35¢
- 10 Desserts
- 12 Pies
- 29 Cookies
- 18 Breads
- 13 Main Dishes
- 18 Cakes

HANDY ORDER BLANK

Mail to: The Pillsbury Company
Box 1531
Minneapolis, Minnesota 55460

Please send me the following:

_____ copies of Best of the Bake-Off   Regular_____ @ $3.95 each

Deluxe_____ @ $4.95 each

_____ cookbook binders @ $1.25 each

_____ copies of Pillsbury's 14th Grand National Cookbook @ $.35 each

I enclose _____ for the above ordered items.

Name_____

Address_____

City_____ State_____ Zip_____

Allow 3 to 4 weeks for delivery.

COOKIES | PAGE 49

Apple Harvest Squares—page 43   Frosted Fruit Jumbles—page 44   Crunchy Date Slices—page 44

Lemon-y Layers—page 46   Chocolate Beau Catchers—page 47   Almond Tosca Bars—page 50

Peanut Drum Cookies—page 52   Peppermint Twists—page 52   Orange-Oatmeal Chews—page 53

Spicy Crinkles—page 55   Peanut Butter Crunchies—page 54   Twin Cinnamon Whirls—page 55

COOKIES

For a crisp cookie, substitute packaged grated coconut for the flaked coconut.

Macaroonies

Junior Third Prize Winner by Judith Ann Carlson, Amery, Wisconsin

BAKE at 325° for 12 to 15 minutes.   MAKES about 3 dozen cookies.

Beat.......... 2 **eggs** with
⅛ teaspoon **salt*** until foamy. Gradually add
¾ cup **sugar**; continue beating until thick and ivory colored, 5 to 7 minutes.

Fold in....... ½ cup **Pillsbury's Best All Purpose Flour*** and
1 tablespoon **Land O'Lakes Butter,** melted.

Stir in........ 2 cups flaked **coconut**
1 cup (6-oz. pkg.) **Nestlé's Semi-Sweet Chocolate Morsels**
1 teaspoon grated **lemon or orange rind** and
1 teaspoon **Burnett's Pure Vanilla.**

Drop......... dough by rounded teaspoonfuls onto lightly greased and floured cookie sheets.

Bake......... at 325° for 12 to 15 minutes until delicately browned. Cool 1 minute; remove from cookie sheet.

**For use with Pillsbury's Best Self-Rising Flour, omit salt.*

Almond Tosca Bars

Senior Winner by Mrs. James C. Conboy, St. Johnsville, New York

BAKE at 375° for 12 minutes, then   MAKES about 2 dozen.
for 10 to 12 minutes.

Cream........ ⅓ cup **Land O'Lakes Butter** with
1 teaspoon grated **lemon rind,** if desired. Add
⅓ cup **sugar** and
½ teaspoon **salt;*** cream well.

Blend in...... 1¼ cups sifted **Pillsbury's Best All Purpose Flour.*** Mixture will be crumbly.

Press......... into bottom of ungreased 8x8 or 11x7-inch pan.

Bake......... at 375° for 12 minutes. Do not brown. Sprinkle with
½ cup **Nestlé's Semi-Sweet Chocolate Morsels.** Let stand 5 minutes; spread. Pour Topping over chocolate. Bake 10 to 12 minutes until golden. Cool; cut into squares.

**For use with Pillsbury's Best Self-Rising Flour, omit salt.*

Almond Tosca Topping

Combine in saucepan ¾ cup chopped almonds, ½ cup sugar, ⅓ cup light cream and ¼ cup Land O'Lakes Butter. Bring to a boil; boil 3 minutes.

COOKIES | PAGE 51

Ginger Boys
Senior Winner by Catherine W. Olds, Brigham City, Utah

BAKE at 325° for 12 to 15 minutes.   MAKES about 2½ dozen cookies.

Sift together... 3¼ cups sifted **Pillsbury's Best All Purpose Flour***
        1 teaspoon **cinnamon**
        ¼ teaspoon **soda**
        ¼ teaspoon **ginger**
        ¼ teaspoon **cloves**

Combine...... in medium saucepan
        1 cup firmly packed **brown sugar**
        ½ cup **honey**
        ¼ cup **applesauce** and
        ¼ cup **shortening**. Bring to a boil; simmer 5 minutes. Cool to lukewarm.

Add......... 1 unbeaten **egg**
        ½ cup ground **almonds** and dry ingredients. Mix well. Chill 6 hours or overnight.

Shape........ scant teaspoonfuls dough into balls for heads. Shape scant teaspoonfuls dough into 4-inch strips for legs and 3-inch strips for arms. Place on greased cookie sheets. Shape as desired. Make eyes and nose from cut raisins and mouth from red cinnamon candies.

Bake......... at 325° for 12 to 15 minutes. Do not brown. Store in covered container 3 to 4 days before serving.

For use with Pillsbury's Best Self-Rising Flour, omit soda.

Walnut Sandwich Cookies
Senior Winner by Mr. Jay M. Smith, Harborcreek, Pennsylvania

BAKE at 350° for 12 to 15 minutes.   MAKES about 3½ dozen.

Cream......... ¾ cup **Land O'Lakes Butter**. Gradually add
        1 cup **sugar** and
        ½ teaspoon **salt,*** creaming well.

Stir in........ ¾ cup chopped **Diamond Black or English Walnuts** and
        1½ to 1¾ cups **Pillsbury's Best All Purpose Flour*** to form a stiff dough.

Shape........ into balls, using a scant teaspoonful for each. Place on ungreased cookie sheets. Flatten with fork which has been dipped in flour.

Bake......... at 350° for 12 to 15 minutes until light golden brown. Cool; place flat-sides of two cookies together with Filling, sandwich-style. Brush tops with Glaze.

For use with Pillsbury's Best Self-Rising Flour, omit salt.

Creamy Filling
Combine 1½ cups sifted confectioners' sugar, ⅓ cup (3-oz. pkg.) cream cheese, 1 tablespoon soft Land O'Lakes Butter and 1 teaspoon grated orange rind. Beat until smooth and of spreading consistency.

Orange Glaze
Combine ¼ cup confectioners' sugar, 1 teaspoon grated orange rind, 4 teaspoons orange juice and 2 drops Burnett's Yellow Food Coloring. Mix well.

- For a smaller cookie, stack 2 cookies together; reserve ½ Vanilla Filling for Chocolate Frosting.
- For Petit Four Cookies, increase milk to ⅓ cup to make a glaze. Frost top allowing glaze to run down sides.

Peanut Drum Cookies

Senior Winner by Mrs. R. J. Graves, Fresno, California

BAKE at 400° for 7 to 10 minutes.　　　　MAKES 3 to 4 dozen.

Sift together...	3 cups sifted **Pillsbury's Best All Purpose Flour*** ½ teaspoon **salt** ½ teaspoon **soda**
Cream.......	1 cup **Land O'Lakes Butter.** Gradually add 1 cup **sugar,** creaming well.
Add.........	1 unbeaten **egg** and 2 teaspoons **Burnett's Pure Vanilla.**
Gradually add..	the dry ingredients; blend well.
Stir in.......	1 cup salted **peanuts,** finely chopped; blend thoroughly. If desired, chill for easier handling.
Roll out......	on floured surface to 1/16 to ⅛-inch thickness. Cut into rounds with floured 2-inch cutter or fancy shaped cutter; place on ungreased cookie sheets.
Bake........	at 400° for 7 to 10 minutes.
Stack.......	3 cookies together with Vanilla Filling. Top with Chocolate Frosting. Arrange 5 **peanut halves** on frosting to form flower.

*For use with Pillsbury's Best Self-Rising Flour, omit salt and soda.

Vanilla Filling

Combine 6 tablespoons soft Land O'Lakes Butter and 1 pound (4 to 4½ cups) sifted confectioners' sugar. Add ¼ cup milk and 1½ teaspoons Burnett's Pure Vanilla. If necessary, thin with milk. Fill cookies, saving about ⅓ of filling for Chocolate Frosting.

Chocolate Frosting

Add 1 cup (6-oz. pkg.) Nestlé's Semi-Sweet Chocolate Morsels, melted, to remaining filling. Blend thoroughly. If necessary, thin with milk.

Any cookie press plate desired may be used to make Peppermint Twists. Added touches—sprinkle with colored sugars or chopped Diamond Walnuts before baking.

Peppermint Twists

Senior Winner by Mrs. Anthony Rezell, Milwaukee, Wisconsin

BAKE at 375° for 8 to 12 minutes.　　　　MAKES about 6 dozen cookies.

Cream.......	1 cup **Land O'Lakes Butter.** Gradually add ¾ cup **sugar,** creaming well.
Blend in......	1 unbeaten **egg** and 1 teaspoon **Burnett's Almond Extract;** beat well.
Add.........	2½ to 3 cups **Pillsbury's Best All Purpose Flour*** gradually to make a soft dough.
Divide.......	dough in half. To one part add ⅛ to ¼ teaspoon **Burnett's Peppermint Extract** and ¼ teaspoon **Burnett's Red or Green Food Coloring.**
Shape.......	about half of each part into a 6x1½-inch roll. Twist together. Fit into a cookie press.

Press.........	small amount of dough onto ungreased cookie sheets, using star plate, to make candy canes 3½ inches long. Repeat with remaining dough.
Bake.........	at 375° for 8 to 12 minutes until delicate brown on edges.

*Pillsbury's Best Self-Rising Flour may be substituted.

Orange-Oatmeal Chews
Junior Winner by Jean Nurse, Anchorage, Alaska

BAKE at 350° for 10 to 12 minutes.   MAKES 2½ dozen cookies.

Toast.........	1 cup quick-cooking **rolled oats** in a shallow pan at 350° for 10 minutes. Cool.
Sift together...	¾ cup **Pillsbury's Best All Purpose Flour*** ½ teaspoon **salt** ½ teaspoon double-acting **baking powder** and ½ teaspoon **soda**. Set aside.
Gradually add..	½ cup **sugar** and ½ cup firmly packed **brown sugar** to ½ cup **shortening**, creaming well.
Blend in......	1 unbeaten **egg** 1 teaspoon **Burnett's Pure Vanilla** and 2 tablespoons grated **orange rind**; beat well.
Stir in........	the dry ingredients, rolled oats and ½ cup chopped **Diamond Walnuts**.
Drop.........	dough by teaspoonfuls, at least 2 inches apart, onto lightly greased cookie sheets.
Bake.........	at 350° for 10 to 12 minutes until golden brown. Cool 1 minute; remove from cookie sheet.

*For use with Pillsbury's Best Self-Rising Flour, omit salt, baking powder and soda.

Candy Surprises
Senior Winner by Mrs. Horace F. Godshall, Collegeville, Pennsylvania

BAKE at 350° for 30 to 35 minutes.   MAKES about 2 dozen bars.

Sift together...	2 cups sifted **Pillsbury's Best All Purpose Flour*** 2 teaspoons double-acting **baking powder** ¼ teaspoon **salt**
Melt.........	½ cup **Land O'Lakes Butter** in saucepan. Remove from heat.
Blend in......	1½ cups firmly packed **brown sugar**.
Add..........	2 unbeaten **eggs** and 1 teaspoon **Burnett's Pure Vanilla**. Beat well.
Stir in........	the dry ingredients.
Spread.......	6 tablespoons (1 tablespoon per bar) **peanut butter** over 6 five-cent **Nestlé's Milk Chocolate Candy Bars**.
Spread.......	half of batter in 9-inch square pan. Place candy bars on batter. Top with remaining batter.
Bake.........	at 350° for 30 to 35 minutes. Cool. Sprinkle with **confectioners' sugar**. Cut into bars.

*For use with Pillsbury's Self-Rising Flour, omit baking powder and salt.

PAGE 54 | COOKIES

Bake Sale Foods—Chocolate Shadows; Peanut Butter Crunchies; Candy Surprises, page 53; Peach Flip, page 74; and Cherry Marble Cake, page 34. Place product in plastic bag and seal. It not only protects the food, but lets the customer see what she is buying.

Chocolate Shadows

Senior Winner by Mrs. Donna Unzelman, Chehalis, Washington

BAKE at 375° for 8 to 10 minutes.   MAKES about 3 dozen cookies.

Melt..........	½ cup **Nestlé's Semi-Sweet Chocolate Morsels**. Stir in ⅛ to ¼ teaspoon **Burnett's Peppermint Extract**. Cool.
Sift together...	1¼ cups sifted **Pillsbury's Best All Purpose Flour*** ¾ teaspoon **soda** and ½ teaspoon **salt**. Set aside.
Gradually add..	½ cup **sugar** and ½ cup firmly packed **brown sugar** to ½ cup **shortening** and ½ cup **peanut butter,** creaming well.
Add..........	1 unbeaten **egg**; mix well.
Blend in......	dry ingredients. Add chocolate. **Stir just to revel.**
Shape........	into balls, using a rounded teaspoonful for each. Place on greased cookie sheets. Flatten with bottom of glass which has been dipped in sugar.
Bake.........	at 375° for 8 to 10 minutes until delicately browned.

*For use with Pillsbury's Best Self-Rising Flour, omit soda and salt.

A special treat for a Valentine's Party! Wrap individual cookies in cellophane and tie with a red ribbon.

Peanut Butter Crunchies

Senior Winner by Mrs. Kenneth F. Allen, Elm Creek, Nebraska

BAKE at 350° for 15 to 20 minutes.   MAKES about 3 dozen bars.

Cream........	½ cup **Land O'Lakes Butter**. Add ½ cup firmly packed **brown sugar,** creaming well.
Add..........	1 cup **Pillsbury's Best All Purpose Flour.*** Press into bottom of greased 9-inch square pan.
Bake.........	at 350° for 15 to 20 minutes until golden brown. Cool.

Crunchie Noodle Topping

Combine......	in top of double boiler 1 cup **peanut butter** ½ cup firmly packed **brown sugar** ¼ cup light **cream** and ½ pound (about 40) **marshmallows** or 5 cups miniature marshmallows. Cook over boiling water until marshmallows are melted.
Add..........	4 cups (5½-oz. can) **chow mein noodles** and ¼ cup cut **maraschino cherries**.
Sprinkle......	½ cup **Nestlé's Semi-Sweet Chocolate Morsels** over base. Spoon topping over chocolate morsels; pat evenly with lightly greased fingers. Cool; cut into squares.

*Pillsbury's Best Self-Rising Flour may be substituted.

COOKIES | PAGE 55

Spicy Crinkles

Junior Winner by Gloria Cassidy, Pittsburgh, Pennsylvania

BAKE at 350° for 10 to 12 minutes.   MAKES about 2½ dozen cookies.

Sift together... 1¼ cups sifted **Pillsbury's Best All Purpose Flour***
- 1 teaspoon **soda**
- 1 teaspoon **cardamom**
- 2½ teaspoons **cinnamon** and
- ½ teaspoon **salt**. Set aside.

Gradually add.. ½ cup **sugar** and
- ¼ cup firmly packed **brown sugar** to
- ½ cup **shortening**, creaming well.

Blend in...... 1 unbeaten **egg** and
- 2 teaspoons **Burnett's Rum Flavor**.

Add.......... ½ cup flaked **coconut** or chopped **Diamond Walnuts** and the dry ingredients; blend well.

Drop......... by teaspoonfuls onto ungreased cookie sheets.

Bake......... at 350° for 10 to 12 minutes until golden brown.

*For use with Pillsbury's Best Self-Rising Flour, decrease soda to ½ teaspoon and omit salt.

Twin Cinnamon Whirls are ideal to serve warm as a petite cinnamon roll for afternoon coffee party, as a luncheon roll or for brunch.

Twin Cinnamon Whirls

Senior Winner by Mrs. Ann Dubas, Woodbury, New Jersey

BAKE at 350° for 20 to 25 minutes.   MAKES 4 dozen cookies.

Sift together... 2¼ cups sifted **Pillsbury's Best All Purpose Flour***
- 2 teaspoons double-acting **baking powder**
- 1 teaspoon **salt**

Cream........ ½ cup **Land O'Lakes Butter**. Add
- ¼ cup **sugar**; cream well.

Add.......... 1 cup creamed **cottage cheese**
- 1 unbeaten **egg** and
- 1 teaspoon **Burnett's Pure Vanilla**; blend well.

Stir in....... dry ingredients; mix well.

Divide....... dough into thirds; flatten and wrap in waxed paper. Chill at least 2 hours.

Combine...... ¾ cup **sugar** and
- 2 to 3 teaspoons **cinnamon**.

Roll out...... one portion, on surface sprinkled with one-third of cinnamon-sugar mixture, to a 12-inch circle. Turn dough over several times to absorb cinnamon-sugar mixture. Brush with
- 1 tablespoon **jelly**, jam or melted **Land O'Lakes Butter**.

Cut.......... into 16 wedges. Roll up, starting with wide end and rolling to point. Cut ¾ of the way through center of wedges. Spread apart; place, cut-side down, on greased cookie sheet. Repeat with remaining dough.

Bake......... at 350° for 20 to 25 minutes. Serve warm or cold.

*For use with Pillsbury's Best Self-Rising Flour, omit baking powder and salt.

PAGE 56 | PIES

Her three young grandsons call Mrs. Arthur P. Grunert of Oklahoma City, Oklahoma, "the best cook in the whole world" and her Orange Dream Pie in this year's Bake-Off explains their conviction.

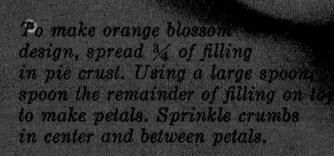

To make orange blossom design, spread ¾ of filling in pie crust. Using a large spoon, spoon the remainder of filling on top to make petals. Sprinkle crumbs in center and between petals.

Orange Dream Pie

Senior Winner by Mrs. Arthur Grunert, Oklahoma City, Oklahoma

BAKE at 375° for 8 to 12 minutes.   MAKES 9-inch pie.

Soften......... ½ cup **Land O'Lakes Butter*** with
3 tablespoons **sugar**.

Add........... 1⅓ cups sifted **Pillsbury's Best All Purpose Flour*** and ¼ teaspoon **salt**. Mix just until a dough will form. (With electric mixer, use low speed.) Place ⅓ cup of the mixture in a small pan for crumb topping.

Press.......... remaining mixture evenly over bottom and sides of a 9-inch piepan. Flute.

Bake.......... at 375° until light golden brown: crumbs 8 to 10 minutes; crust 10 to 12 minutes. Cool.

Orange Cheese Filling

Combine....... ¼ cup undiluted frozen **orange juice** and
1 envelope (1 tablespoon) unflavored **gelatin** in top of double boiler.

Add........... 3 **egg whites**
½ cup **sugar** and
¼ teaspoon **cream of tartar**. Cook over boiling water, beating constantly, with electric mixer or rotary beater, until stiff peaks form. Set aside.

Combine....... in medium saucepan
¼ cup undiluted frozen **orange juice**
3 **egg yolks**
½ cup **sugar**
1 teaspoon **Burnett's Pure Vanilla** and
¼ teaspoon **salt**. Beat with electric mixer or rotary beater until light. Cook, stirring constantly, until smooth and thick. Remove from heat.

Add........... 1 cup (8-oz. pkg.) **cream cheese**; beat until smooth. Fold into gelatin-egg white mixture. Chill until thickened but not set, about 30 minutes.

Beat.......... 1 cup **whipping cream** until thick; fold into gelatin mixture.

Spoon......... into baked shell. Sprinkle with reserved crumbs. Chill at least 2 hours.

*For use with Pillsbury's Best Self-Rising Flour, use unsalted butter and omit salt, or use your favorite pastry.

If desired, substitute sliced pineapple for crushed pineapple. Cut 4 slices into 12 wedges each and arrange on custard after first baking. Top with coconut mixture and broil.

Pineapple Brulé Pie

Senior Winner by Carol Ann Johnson, Alta, Iowa

BAKE at 400° for 25 to 30 minutes.   MAKES 9-inch pie.

Sift together...	1 cup sifted **Pillsbury's Best All Purpose Flour*** and ½ teaspoon **salt** into mixing bowl.
Cut in.........	⅓ cup **shortening** until particles are fine.
Sprinkle......	3 to 4 tablespoons cold **water** over mixture while tossing and stirring lightly with fork. Add water to driest particles, pushing lumps to side, until dough is just moist enough to hold together.
Form..........	into a ball. Flatten to ½-inch thickness; smooth edges.
Roll out.......	on floured surface to a circle 1½ inches larger than inverted 9-inch piepan. Fit into pan. Fold edge to form a standing rim; flute.

Pineapple Custard Filling

Drain.........	1 can (8¾ oz.) crushed **pineapple**; reserve juice.
Combine......	in mixing bowl 3 slightly beaten **eggs** ½ cup **sugar** 1 teaspoon **Burnett's Pure Vanilla** ¼ teaspoon **salt** ¼ teaspoon **nutmeg** and reserved pineapple juice (⅓ cup).
Gradually add..	2 cups hot light **cream**; mix well. Pour into lined pan.
Bake..........	at 400° for 25 to 30 minutes until knife inserted halfway between the center and edge of filling comes out clean. Top with crushed pineapple (⅔ cup) and Coconut Topping. Cover edge with foil.
Broil.........	1 to 2 minutes, watching carefully, until mixture bubbles and begins to brown. Cool.

*For use with Pillsbury's Best Self-Rising Flour, omit salt.

Coconut Topping

Combine ½ cup flaked coconut, ¼ cup firmly packed brown sugar, 3 tablespoons cream and 2 tablespoons melted Land O'Lakes Butter.

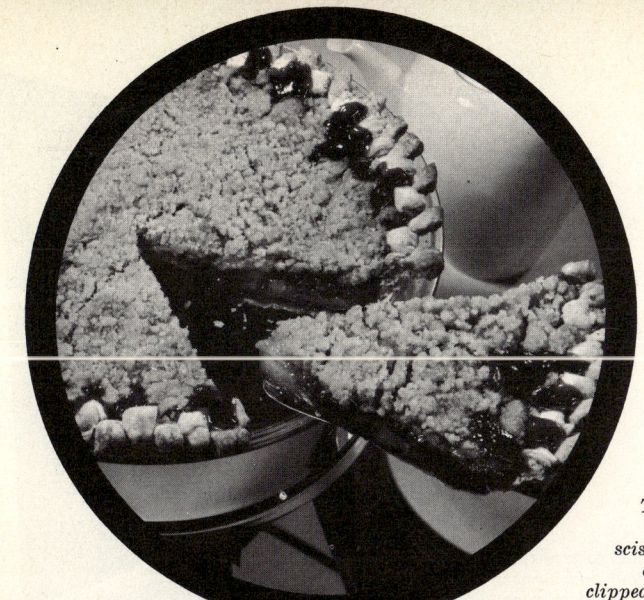

To make leaf edge, form a high standing rim. With scissors, clip rim at an angle every ¼ inch. Press down clipped rim to the right and left.

Melba Streusel Pie

Senior Winner by Mrs. Gerald V. Stoeckel, Minneapolis, Minnesota

BAKE at 375° for 30 to 35 minutes, then for 10 to 15 minutes.   MAKES 9-inch pie.

Sift together...	1 cup sifted **Pillsbury's Best All Purpose Flour*** and ½ teaspoon **salt** into mixing bowl.
Cut in........	⅓ cup **shortening** until particles are fine.
Sprinkle......	3 to 4 tablespoons cold **water** over mixture while tossing and stirring lightly with fork. Add water to driest particles, pushing lumps to side, until dough is just moist enough to hold together.
Form.........	into a ball. Flatten to ½-inch thickness; smooth edges.
Roll out.......	on floured surface to a circle 1½ inches larger than inverted 9-inch piepan. Fit into pan. Fold edge to form a standing rim; flute.

Fruit Filling

Thaw........	1 package (10 oz.) frozen sliced **peaches** and 1 package (10 oz.) frozen **raspberries**.
Combine......	¼ cup **sugar** 3 tablespoons **corn starch** and ¼ teaspoon **cinnamon**; add to thawed fruit.
Sprinkle......	1 tablespoon **lemon juice** over fruit; mix well. Turn into pastry-lined pan.
Bake.........	at 375° for 30 to 35 minutes or until filling is partially set in the center. Sprinkle with Streusel Topping. Bake 10 to 15 minutes until golden brown.

**For use with Pillsbury's Best Self-Rising Flour, omit salt.*

Streusel Topping

Cut ¼ cup Land O'Lakes Butter into mixture of ¾ cup Pillsbury's Best All Purpose Flour and ½ cup firmly packed brown sugar.

PIES

A pastry cloth and a stockinet covered rolling pin reduce the amount of flour and number of strokes needed to roll dough—thus more tender pie crust.

Mocha Frappé Pie

Senior Winner by Mrs. Julie Conners, Stanford, California

BAKE at 375° for 12 to 15 minutes.   MAKES 9-inch pie.

Sift together...	1 cup sifted **Pillsbury's Best All Purpose Flour*** 2 tablespoons **sugar** and ½ teaspoon **salt** into mixing bowl.
Cut in........	⅓ cup **shortening** until particles are fine.
Combine......	1 **egg yolk** and enough **water** to make ¼ cup. Sprinkle over flour mixture while tossing and stirring with fork. Add liquid to driest particles, pushing lumps to side, until dough is moist enough to hold together.
Form.........	into a ball. Flatten to ½-inch thickness; smooth edges.
Roll out......	on floured surface to a circle 1½ inches larger than inverted 9-inch piepan. Fit loosely into pan. Fold edge to form rim; flute. Prick generously with fork.
Bake.........	at 375° for 12 to 15 minutes until golden brown. Cool.

Chocolate Filling

Combine......	in top of double boiler ½ pound (about 40) **marshmallows** ¼ cup **sugar** 2 teaspoons **Nescafé Instant Coffee** and ½ cup **evaporated milk.** Cook over boiling water, stirring occasionally, until marshmallows are melted.
Stir in.......	1 cup (6-oz. pkg.) **Nestlé's Semi-Sweet Chocolate Morsels.** Cool slightly. Spread ¾ cup in bottom of baked shell.
Beat.........	1 cup **whipping cream** until thick. Fold in remaining chocolate mixture.
Spoon........	over chocolate layer. Chill at least 2 hours before serving. If desired, serve with whipped cream.

*For use with Pillsbury's Best Self-Rising Flour, omit salt.

For a light fluffy chiffon pie the gelatin mixture should be chilled just until it mounds slightly when dropped from a spoon. Spoon the filling into the pie carefully then chill pie until firm.

Bonanza Banana Pie

Junior Winner by Austin Andrew Marks, Camden, New Jersey

BAKE at 450° for 10 to 12 minutes.*   MAKES 9-inch pie.

Sift together...	1 cup sifted **Pillsbury's Best All Purpose Flour*** and ½ teaspoon **salt** into mixing bowl.
Cut in........	⅓ cup **shortening** until particles are fine.
Sprinkle......	3 to 4 tablespoons cold **water** over mixture while tossing and stirring lightly with fork. Add water to driest particles, pushing lumps to side, until dough is just moist enough to hold together.
Form.........	into a ball. Flatten to ½-inch thickness; smooth edges.
Roll out......	on floured surface to a circle 1½ inches larger than inverted 9-inch piepan. Fit loosely into pan. Fold edge to form a standing rim; flute. Prick generously with fork.
Bake.........	at 450° for 10 to 12 minutes until golden brown.

Banana Filling

Combine......	1 envelope (1 tablespoon) unflavored **gelatin** ¼ cup **sugar** and ¼ teaspoon **salt** in top of double boiler.
Add..........	¾ cup **milk** and 2 **egg yolks.** Cook over boiling water, stirring constantly, until gelatin dissolves and mixture coats a metal spoon. Chill until thickened but not set.
Mash.........	2 medium (about 1 cup) **bananas** with 1 tablespoon **lemon juice**; stir into gelatin mixture.
Beat.........	2 **egg whites** until soft mounds form. Gradually add 2 tablespoons **sugar,** beating until stiff, glossy peaks form. Fold into gelatin mixture.
Beat.........	1 cup **whipping cream** until thick. Fold gently into gelatin mixture. Chill until mixture is thickened but not set.
Spoon........	into baked shell. Chill until firm, at least 4 hours. If desired, garnish with **Diamond Walnut Halves.**

*For use with Pillsbury's Best Self-Rising Flour, omit salt. Bake 8 to 10 minutes.

Little Surprise Pies

French Pear P[ie]

Little Surprise Pies

Senior Winner by Mrs. M. E. Walcott, Columbus, Wisconsin

BAKE at 350° for 20 to 25 minutes.   MAKES 18.

Cream........	½ cup **Land O'Lakes Butter**. Add ⅓ cup **sugar**, creaming well.
Gradually add..	1¼ cups sifted **Pillsbury's Best All Purpose Flour**,* mixing to form a dough.
Press.........	scant tablespoonfuls of dough into bottom and ¾ inch up sides of paper baking cups. Place in muffin cups.
Combine......	¾ cup firmly packed **brown sugar** 1 slightly beaten **egg** and 1 teaspoon **Burnett's Rum Flavor**; stir until well blended. Spoon about 2 teaspoonfuls into each tart.
Top with......	a solid **chocolate rum wafer** or 6 **Nestlé's Semi-Sweet Chocolate Morsels**.
Combine......	1⅓ cups flaked or packaged grated **coconut** with ½ cup **sweetened condensed milk**. Spoon over wafers.
Bake.........	at 350° for 20 to 25 minutes until lightly browned.

*Pillsbury's Best Self-Rising Flour may be substituted.

French Pear Pie

Senior Winner by Mrs. Ernest Davenport, Newland, North Carolina

BAKE at 400° for 25 to 30 minutes.   MAKES 9-inch pie.

Sift together...	1 cup sifted **Pillsbury's Best All Purpose Flour*** and ½ teaspoon **salt** into mixing bowl.
Cut in........	⅓ cup **shortening** until particles are fine.
Sprinkle......	3 to 4 tablespoons cold **water** over mixture while stirring with fork until dough is moist enough to hold together.
Form.........	into a ball. Flatten to ½-inch thickness; smooth edges.
Roll out.......	on floured surface to a circle 1½ inches larger than inverted 9-inch piepan. Fit into pan. Flute edge.

Sour Cream Pear Filling

Drain.........	1 can (1 lb. 13 oz.) **pear halves**. Arrange pears (7 or 8), cut-side up, in pastry-lined pan.
Combine......	3 tablespoons **flour** ½ cup **sugar** ¼ teaspoon **ginger** and 1½ cups dairy **sour cream**; mix well. Pour over pears.
Combine......	½ cup **Pillsbury's Best All Purpose Flour** ¼ cup firmly packed **brown sugar** and ½ teaspoon **nutmeg** in mixing bowl. Cut in ¼ cup **Land O'Lakes Butter**; sprinkle over filling.
Bake.........	at 400° for 25 to 30 minutes until golden brown.

*For use with Pillsbury's Best Self-Rising Flour, omit salt.

PIES | PAGE **63**

Southern Pineapple Tarts

Apple 'n Cheese Tarts

Apple 'n Cheese Tarts

Senior Winner by Winona Zeigler, Pittsburgh, Pennsylvania

BAKE at 400° for 12 to 15 minutes. MAKES about 2 dozen.

Combine......	2 cups sifted **Pillsbury's Best All Purpose Flour*** 2 cups shredded **Cheddar cheese** and ½ teaspoon **salt** in mixing bowl.
Cut in........	½ cup **Land O'Lakes Butter** until particles are fine.
Sprinkle......	⅓ cup **milk** over mixture while stirring with fork until dough holds together.
Form.........	into a ball. Wrap in waxed paper. Chill ½ hour.
Roll out.......	on floured surface to ⅛-inch thickness. Cut into rounds with floured 3-inch cutter or fancy shaped cutter. Place half of rounds on ungreased cookie sheets.
Place.........	a rounded teaspoonful Filling in center of each. Cut a cross in remaining rounds; place over Filling. Seal.
Bake.........	at 400° for 12 to 15 minutes until light golden brown. (Dough and Filling may be refrigerated and baked as needed.)

*For use with Pillsbury's Best Self-Rising Flour, omit salt.

Apple Filling

Combine 1 cup canned apple pie filling, cut in small pieces, and ¼ cup raisins.

Southern Pineapple Tarts

Senior Winner by Mrs. Ted George, Pemberville, Ohio

BAKE at 350° for 30 to 35 minutes. MAKES 12.

Cream........	½ cup soft **Land O'Lakes Butter** with 2 tablespoons **sugar** and ⅓ cup (3-oz. pkg.) **cream cheese**.
Gradually add..	1½ cups sifted **Pillsbury's Best All Purpose Flour;*** mix thoroughly. Form into a ball. Chill 30 minutes.
Press.........	dough into bottom and up sides of muffin cups.
Sprinkle......	½ cup chopped **pecans** in bottom of pastry-lined cups.
Combine......	2 slightly beaten **eggs** 1 cup firmly packed **brown sugar** ⅔ cup (8¾-oz. can) drained crushed **pineapple** and 2 tablespoons **Land O'Lakes Butter**, melted.
Spoon........	into pastry-lined cups, filling ¾ full. Sprinkle with ¼ cup chopped **pecans**.
Bake.........	at 350° for 30 to 35 minutes until golden brown. Cool at least 15 minutes before removing from pans.

*Self-rising flour is not recommended for use in this recipe.

To make a fluted edge, form a high standing rim. Place right index finger inside rim; make flutes every half inch by pushing pastry into "V" with left thumb and index finger on outside of rim. Pinch flutes for clean edges.

Becky's Fruit Pie

Junior Winner by Becky Jelle, Hibbing, Minnesota

BAKE at 400° for 30 to 40 minutes,* then at 350° for 12 to 15 minutes.

MAKES 9-inch pie.

Sift together... 1 cup sifted **Pillsbury's Best All Purpose Flour*** and ½ teaspoon **salt** into mixing bowl.

Cut in......... ⅓ cup **shortening** until particles are fine.

Sprinkle....... 3 to 4 tablespoons cold **water** over mixture while tossing and stirring lightly with fork. Add water to driest particles, pushing lumps to side until dough is just moist enough to hold together.

Form.......... into a ball. Flatten to ½-inch thickness; smooth edges.

Roll out....... on floured surface to a circle 1½ inches larger than inverted 9-inch piepan. Fit into pan. Fold edge to form a standing rim. Flute.

Fruit Filling

Drain......... 1 can (1 lb.) **peach slices** and 1 can (1 lb.) **apricot halves**; reserve ¾ cup juice.

Combine...... 2 tablespoons **Pillsbury's Best All Purpose Flour** ¼ cup **sugar** and ½ teaspoon **cinnamon** in medium saucepan. Gradually add reserved juice and 1 teaspoon **lemon juice**, blending until smooth. Stir in 1 medium **apple**, pared and finely chopped. Cook over medium heat, stirring constantly, until thick.

Stir in........ ½ cup **raisins** and drained fruit. Turn into pastry-lined pan.

Bake......... at 400° for 30 to 40 minutes until crust is golden brown. Spread Meringue over filling, sealing edges.

Bake......... at 350° for 12 to 15 minutes until lightly browned.

*For use with Pillsbury's Best Self-Rising Flour, omit salt. Bake at 400° for 25 to 30 minutes.

Meringue

Beat 3 **egg whites** with ¼ teaspoon **cream of tartar** and ½ teaspoon **cinnamon** until soft mounds form. Gradually add 6 tablespoons **sugar**; beat well after each addition. Continue beating until meringue stands in stiff peaks.

If some areas of pie crust brown quicker than others, cover these areas with foil for remaining baking time.

Apple ála Cream Pie

Junior Winner by Ardene Wiebbecke, Clutier, Iowa

BAKE at 400° for 40 to 50 minutes.*   MAKES 9-inch pie.

Sift together...	1 cup sifted **Pillsbury's Best All Purpose Flour*** and ½ teaspoon **salt** into mixing bowl.
Cut in.........	⅓ cup **shortening** until particles are fine.
Sprinkle......	3 to 4 tablespoons cold **water** over mixture while tossing and stirring lightly with fork. Add water to driest particles, pushing lumps to side, until dough is just moist enough to hold together.
Form.........	into a ball. Flatten to ½-inch thickness; smooth edges.
Roll out.......	on floured surface to circle 1½ inches larger than inverted 9-inch piepan. Fit into pan. Fold edge to form rim; flute.
Sprinkle......	1 tablespoon **bread crumbs** or finely chopped almonds over bottom of pastry-lined pan.

Apple-Custard Filling

Combine......	4 cups pared, sliced **apples** (about 4 medium) ⅓ cup **sugar** and 2 tablespoons **flour**. Arrange in pastry-lined pan. Cut a circle of foil to fit over filling. Press firmly over filling. (Do not cover pastry.)
Bake.........	at 400° for 25 to 35 minutes until almost tender.
Combine......	2 slightly beaten **eggs** 1 cup **cream** ½ teaspoon **cinnamon** ¼ teaspoon **nutmeg** and ¼ cup **sugar**. Pour over apples. Sprinkle with Topping.
Bake.........	at 400° for 15 to 20 minutes or until metal knife inserted about halfway between the center and outside of filling comes out clean.

*For use with Pillsbury's Best Self-Rising Flour, omit salt. Bake at 375°.

Crumb Topping

Combine 3 tablespoons sugar, 2 tablespoons bread crumbs or finely chopped almonds and 2 tablespoons Land O'Lakes Butter to make a crumb mixture.

PAGE **66** | DESSERTS

A travel buff and a cook who has no favorite recipes—likes making them *all*—is Mrs. Leonard Manske of Franklin, Wisconsin. She traveled to California to bake her own creation for Bake-Off judges—who awarded it the $1,000 Best of Class Pies and Desserts prize.

DESSERTS | PAGE 67

If you don't have three 9-inch layer pans, hold ⅓ of dough and topping in refrigerator. Bake as soon as pan is available. For a filling with a subtle sour cream flavor, beat ½ cup whipping cream and combine with 1 cup sour cream. Save some filling to decorate the top.

Sunday Special Torte

Senior Best of Class Winner by Mrs. Leonard Manske, Franklin, Wisconsin

BAKE at 350° for 35 to 40 minutes.   SERVES 10 to 12.

Cream.......	1 cup **Land O'Lakes Butter**. Add ½ cup **sugar**, creaming well.
Blend in......	5 **egg yolks** 2 tablespoons **milk** 1 teaspoon **Burnett's Pure Vanilla** ½ teaspoon double-acting **baking powder*** and ½ teaspoon **salt**; beat well.
Stir in........	2 cups sifted **Pillsbury's Best All Purpose Flour.***
Spread.......	evenly into bottoms of three 9-inch round layer pans, greased on bottoms. Spread ⅓ cup **raspberry preserves** on each layer to within 1 inch of edge.
Beat.........	5 **egg whites** and ¼ teaspoon **salt** until slight mounds form. Gradually add 1 cup **sugar**, beating well after each addition. Continue beating until stiff peaks form.
Fold in.......	1⅓ cups (3½-oz. can) flaked **coconut** and 1 teaspoon **Burnett's Pure Vanilla**. Spread over preserves.
Bake.........	at 350° for 35 to 40 minutes until light golden brown. Cool 15 minutes; remove from pans. Cool completely.
Spread.......	2 cups dairy **sour cream** between layers, leaving top plain. Chill several hours or overnight.

*For use with Pillsbury's Best Self-Rising Flour, omit baking powder and salt.

Two packages (1 lb. each) frozen rhubarb may be substituted for the fresh rhubarb. Decrease the 1½ cups water to ¾ cup and the sugar to ½ cup.

Rhubarb Dessert Dumplings

Senior Winner by Mrs. Theodore Eckroth, Bloomsburg, Pennsylvania

STEAM 20 minutes.   SERVES 6.

Combine......	in 8-inch skillet or large saucepan
	4 cups **rhubarb**, cut in 1-inch pieces
	1½ cups **water**
	¼ cup **red cinnamon candies**
	1 to 3 drops **Burnett's Red Food Coloring**, if desired, and
	1 cup **sugar**. Bring to boil; simmer 5 minutes.
Combine......	¼ cup **corn starch** and
	½ cup cold **water**. Stir into rhubarb sauce. Boil 1 minute.
Sift together...	into mixing bowl
	1 cup sifted **Pillsbury's Best All Purpose Flour***
	¼ cup **sugar**
	1½ teaspoons **double-acting baking powder**
	¼ teaspoon **salt**
Cut in........	2 tablespoons **Land O'Lakes Butter** until fine.
Add..........	½ cup **milk** and
	½ teaspoon **Burnett's Pure Vanilla**; stir until dry particles are moistened.
Drop.........	by tablespoonfuls onto hot rhubarb sauce. Cover.
Steam........	20 minutes. Serve warm.

**For use with Pillsbury's Best Self-Rising Flour, omit baking powder and salt. Decrease milk to ⅛ cup.*

DESSERTS | PAGE 69

An easy dessert that is special enough for company and easy enough for a family dessert.

Pineapple Dessert Pie

Senior Winner by Mrs. Don J. Stevens, Overland Park, Kansas

BAKE at 325° for 20 to 25 minutes. SERVES 6 to 8.

Sift together... 1¼ cups sifted **Pillsbury's Best All Purpose Flour***
          ½ teaspoon **soda**
          ½ teaspoon **salt**

Combine...... ½ cup **Land O'Lakes Butter**
          ⅓ cup **sugar**
          1 teaspoon **Burnett's Pure Vanilla** and
          1 unbeaten **egg**. Add dry ingredients; blend well. Spread in bottom of ungreased 9-inch piepan.

Bake......... at 325° for 20 to 25 minutes until golden brown. Cool.

Pineapple Filling

Beat......... 1 cup **whipping cream** until thick.
Fold in....... 1 cup **miniature marshmallows**
          1 cup (12-oz. jar) **pineapple preserves**
          1 teaspoon grated **lemon rind**

Cut.......... cake in half horizontally to make 2 thin layers. Place bottom layer in piepan. Spread with half of filling. Top with remaining layer and filling. Sprinkle with chopped **Diamond Walnuts**. Chill at least 3 hours.

**Self-rising flour is not recommended for use in this recipe.*

DESSERTS

A festive dessert for a European meal. It's a make-ahead dessert, too. Strawberries can be substituted for the raspberries.

Raspberry Continental

Senior Winner by Mrs. Charles R. Hulls, Columbus, Ohio

BAKE at 350° for 30 to 35 minutes.   SERVES 9.

- Cream......... ½ cup **Land O'Lakes Butter.** Gradually add 1 cup **sugar,** creaming well.
- Add.......... 1 unbeaten **egg**
  ¼ cup **milk**
  1 teaspoon **Burnett's Pure Vanilla** and
  ½ teaspoon **salt.**
- Stir in........ 1¼ cups sifted **Pillsbury's Best All Purpose Flour*** and ¼ cup toasted blanched **almonds,** chopped.
- Turn.......... into 8-inch square pan, greased on bottom.
- Bake.......... at 350° for 30 to 35 minutes. Remove from pan. Cool. Cut in half horizontally with sharp knife, to make 2 thin layers. Spread bottom layer with Butter Filling and then Raspberry Filling. Top with second layer, then whipped cream. Chill at least 4 hours.

Raspberry and Butter Filling

- Combine...... in saucepan
  ¼ cup **sugar** and
  2 tablespoons **corn starch.** Add
  1 package (10 oz.) frozen **red raspberries.** Cook, stirring constantly, until thick. Cool completely.
- Cream......... ½ cup **Land O'Lakes Butter;** gradually add 1½ cups sifted **confectioners' sugar,** creaming well.
- Add.......... 1 unbeaten **egg;** beat until fluffy.

*Self-rising flour is not recommended for use in this recipe.

Whipped Cream

Beat ¾ cup whipping cream until thick. Stir in 3 tablespoons sugar and ½ cup chopped Diamond Walnuts. Continue beating until stiff.

DESSERTS | PAGE 71

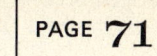

Crepes or thin pancakes make an easy dessert, because they can be made early and then heated just before serving. Pancakes, such as these are fun to serve for Sunday brunch or lunch.

Apple Dessert Pancakes

Junior Winner by Cynthia Kobashigawa, Honolulu, Hawaii

BAKE at medium high heat (375° F.).   MAKES 12 to 15 crepes. (Serves 6 to 8.)

Combine...... 4 cups pared, thinly sliced **apples** (4 medium) with
¼ cup **sugar** and
1 teaspoon **cinnamon** in saucepan. Cover; cook until apples are tender.

Combine...... in small mixing bowl
2 beaten **eggs**
1 cup **milk**
½ teaspoon **Burnett's Pure Vanilla** and
3 tablespoons **Land O'Lakes Butter**, melted.

Stir in........ ½ cup **Pillsbury's Best All Purpose Flour*** and
½ teaspoon **salt**.

Heat......... lightly greased skillet over medium high heat.

Pour......... batter, 2 tablespoons at a time, into skillet. Tilt pan to make a 6-inch round, thin pancake. Brown about one minute; turn and brown on other side.

Place......... about one tablespoonful apple mixture on each; roll up and place in a 12x8-inch baking dish.

Combine...... ½ cup firmly packed **brown sugar**
1 teaspoon grated **orange rind** and
⅓ cup **orange juice**. Sprinkle over pancakes.

Broil......... 5 inches from heat, watching carefully, 2 to 5 minutes until golden brown and pancakes are hot. Serve immediately with **sour cream**.

*For use with Pillsbury's Best Self-Rising Flour, omit salt.

An ideal dessert to serve at your next dessert party.
Note: This moist cake is also a good lunch box dessert.

Easy Hawaiian Torte

Junior Second Prize Winner by Linda Jean Henson, Monte Vista, Colorado

BAKE at 350° for 35 to 40 minutes.   SERVES 9.

Sift together...	1½ cups sifted **Pillsbury's Best All Purpose Flour***
	1 teaspoon **soda**
	1 teaspoon **salt**
Cream........	½ cup **Land O'Lakes Butter**. Gradually add
	1 cup **sugar**, creaming well.
Add..........	1 unbeaten **egg**
	1 cup (8¾-oz. can) undrained crushed **pineapple** and
	1 teaspoon **Burnett's Pure Vanilla**; mix well.
Stir in........	the dry ingredients.
Turn.........	into 9-inch square pan, greased and floured on bottom.
Combine......	½ cup flaked or chopped shredded **coconut** and
	½ cup firmly packed **brown sugar**; sprinkle over batter.
Bake.........	at 350° for 35 to 40 minutes until cake springs back when touched lightly in center. If desired, serve warm or cold with whipped cream or ice cream.

*For use with Pillsbury's Best Self-Rising Flour, omit soda and salt.

DESSERTS | PAGE **73**

An elegant make-ahead dessert for a ladies luncheon. Whipping cream beats best if it is cold; it's a good practice to chill the bowl and beaters.

Chocolate Cream Torte

Senior Winner by Mrs. Irma M. Joyce, St. Louis, Missouri

BAKE at 300° for 25 to 30 minutes.   SERVES 6 to 8.

Beat.......... 8 **egg whites** (1 cup) with
1 teaspoon **Burnett's Almond Extract**
½ teaspoon **cream of tartar** and
½ teaspoon **salt*** until soft peaks form. Gradually add
⅔ cup **sugar**. Continue beating until very stiff.

Fold in....... ¾ cup **Pillsbury's Best All Purpose Flour***
⅓ cup **sugar** and
½ cup flaked **coconut**, using wire whip or rubber spatula.

Spread....... meringue on greased and floured cookie sheets to make three 8-inch circles and one 2-inch circle.

Bake.......... at 300° for 25 to 30 minutes until lightly browned. Remove from sheet immediately. Cool.

Melt.......... 1 cup (6-oz. pkg.) **Nestlé's Semi-Sweet Chocolate Morsels** and
1 cup **miniature marshmallows** in
⅔ cup **evaporated milk** in top of double boiler over boiling water. Chill.

Beat.......... 1 cup **whipping cream** until thick. Fold into chocolate.

Stack......... large layers, spreading filling between and on top. Top with small layer. Chill 6 to 8 hours.

*For use with Pillsbury's Best Self-Rising Flour, omit salt.

BREADS

Mrs. Christine G. Potter of Merion Station, Pennsylvania, modernized an old Danish sweet dough recipe that she learned as a child to create the bread which won the $3,000 prize for first place in the senior division.

Plan ahead. Freeze one coffee cake. To freeze, cool completely, then wrap, label and freeze.

Peach Flip

Senior First Prize Winner by Mrs. Christine Potter, Merion Station, Pennsylvania

BAKE at 350° for 20 to 25 minutes.   MAKES 2 coffee cakes.

Soften........ 2 packets **Red Star Special Active Dry Yeast** (or 2 cakes Red Star Compressed Yeast) in
½ cup warm **water.**

Combine...... in mixing bowl
½ cup **sugar**
½ cup **Land O'Lakes Butter**
½ cup hot scalded **milk** and
2 teaspoons **salt.*** Stir to melt butter. Cool to lukewarm.

Blend in...... 3 unbeaten **eggs** and the softened yeast.

Gradually add.. 5 to 5½ cups **Pillsbury's Best All Purpose Flour*** to form a stiff dough.

Knead........ on floured surface until smooth and satiny, 3 to 5 minutes. Place in greased bowl; cover.

Let rise....... in warm place (85° to 90° F.) until light and doubled in size, 1 to 1½ hours.

Combine...... ⅔ cup **sugar**
2 teaspoons **cinnamon** and
1 cup (4-oz. can) **Diamond Walnuts,** chopped. Set aside.

Roll out....... half of dough on lightly floured surface to a 20x10-inch rectangle. Spread with
2 tablespoons soft **Land O'Lakes Butter** and
¼ cup **peach or apricot preserves.** Sprinkle with half the cinnamon-sugar mixture.

Roll up....... starting with 20-inch side. Seal edge and ends. Place seam-side down on greased cookie sheet, curving ends to make "U" shape. With scissors, make cut down center, ⅓ of the way through roll, to within 2 inches of ends. Repeat with remaining dough.

Let rise....... in warm place until light, about 30 minutes.

Spoon........ ¼ cup **peach preserves** down center of each.

Bake......... at 350° for 20 to 25 minutes until golden brown. Frost.

*For use with Pillsbury's Best Self-Rising Flour, omit salt.

Vanilla Glaze

Combine 1 cup sifted confectioners' sugar, 1 teaspoon Burnett's Pure Vanilla and 2 to 3 teaspoons milk.

BREADS | PAGE 75

BREADS

If you don't have a 15x10x1-inch jelly roll pan, the coffee cake may be baked in two 9-inch square pans.

European Coffee Cake

Senior Winner by Mrs. Pete Schmunk, Bayard, Nebraska

BAKE at 350° for 30 to 40 minutes.   MAKES 15x10-inch coffee cake.

Soften........ 2 packets **Red Star Special Active Dry Yeast** (or 2 cakes Red Star Compressed Yeast) in
¼ cup warm **water**.

Combine...... in mixing bowl
½ cup hot scalded **milk**
⅓ cup **sugar**
¼ cup **shortening**
1½ teaspoons **salt*** and
½ teaspoon **Burnett's Almond Extract**. Cool to lukewarm.

Blend in...... 1 unbeaten **egg** and the softened yeast.

Gradually add.. 2 to 2½ cups **Pillsbury's Best All Purpose Flour*** to make a soft dough; beat well. (For first additions of flour, use mixer.) Cover.

Let rise....... in warm place (85° to 90° F.) until light and doubled in size, about 1½ hours.

Pat.......... into well-greased 15x10x1-inch pan. Spread with 1 can (1 lb. 5 oz.) **cherry pie filling**.

Combine...... ½ cup dairy **sour cream**
1 unbeaten **egg**
2 tablespoons **sugar**
¼ teaspoon **Burnett's Almond Extract** and
⅛ teaspoon **salt**. Drizzle around cherries.

Let rise....... in warm place until light, about 30 minutes. Sprinkle with Topping.

Bake......... at 350° for 30 to 40 minutes.

*For use with Pillsbury's Best Self-Rising Flour, omit salt.

Sugar Crumb Topping

Cut ½ cup Land O'Lakes **Butter** into 1 cup Pillsbury's Best All Purpose **Flour** and ¼ cup **sugar** until particles are the size of small peas.

BREADS | PAGE 77

Any flavor of jam may be used. Or, try a prepared fruit pie filling.

Daisy Breakfast Cake

Senior Winner by Mrs. Frank Newby, Huntington, West Virginia

BAKE at 350° for 15 to 20 minutes.   MAKES 3 coffee cakes.

Soften......... 1 packet **Red Star Special Active Dry Yeast** (or 1 cake Red Star Compressed Yeast) in ½ cup warm **water**.

Combine...... ½ cup **Pillsbury Mashed Potato Flakes** and ½ cup hot **water** in mixing bowl; beat until fluffy.

Stir in........ ⅓ cup **instant nonfat dry milk**
⅓ cup **sugar**
¼ cup **Land O'Lakes Butter**
1 beaten **egg** (reserve 1 tablespoon for glaze)
1 teaspoon **salt*** and the softened yeast.

Gradually add..2½ to 3 cups **Pillsbury's Best All Purpose Flour*** to form a stiff dough, beating well after each addition. Cover.

Let rise....... in warm place (85° to 90° F.) until light and doubled in size, about 1 hour.

Divide........ dough into thirds. Roll out each to an 11-inch circle. Place on greased cookie sheets. With scissors, make diagonal cuts around outside edges 1 inch apart and 1½ inches deep. Alternate cut pieces, bringing one to center and next to outside, curving slightly.

Combine...... 1 tablespoon **milk** with reserved egg. Brush over petals.

Let rise....... in warm place until light, 45 to 60 minutes.

Spread........ ⅓ cup **peach preserves or pie filling** in center of each. (Apricot, cherry or other flavors may be used.)

Bake......... at 350° for 15 to 20 minutes. If desired, frost petals with a confectioners' sugar icing. Sprinkle chopped **Diamond Walnuts** over the centers.

*For use with Pillsbury's Best Self-Rising Flour, omit salt.

BREADS

Lemon Raisin Rolls
Senior Winner by Mrs. Ruby Westmoreland, Lott, Texas

BAKE at 350° for 20 to 25 minutes.   MAKES 1½ to 2 dozen.

Soften........	1 packet **Red Star Special Active Dry Yeast** (or 1 cake Red Star Compressed Yeast) in
	¼ cup warm **water**.
Combine......	in mixing bowl
	1½ cups (12-oz. carton) creamed **cottage cheese**
	1 cup **raisins**
	¾ cup **sweetened condensed milk**
	¼ cup **Land O'Lakes Butter**, melted
	1 unbeaten **egg**
	2 tablespoons grated **lemon rind**
	1½ teaspoons **salt*** and the softened yeast.
Gradually add..	2½ to 2¾ cups **Pillsbury's Best All Purpose Flour*** to form a soft dough; beat well. (For first additions of flour, use mixer.) Cover.
Let rise.......	in warm place (85° to 90° F.) until light, about 1 hour.
Fill..........	well-greased muffin cups two-thirds full. Cover.
Let rise.......	in warm place until light, 45 to 60 minutes. Brush with
	¼ cup **Land O'Lakes Butter**, melted. Sprinkle with **sugar**.
Bake.........	at 350° for 20 to 25 minutes until golden brown. Serve warm.

*For use with Pillsbury's Best Self-Rising Flour, omit salt.

Triple Treat Cloverleafs
Junior Winner by Jane Blackwelder, Crossville, Alabama

Bake at 450° for 10 to 12 minutes.   MAKES 1 dozen rolls.

Soften........	1 packet **Red Star Special Active Dry Yeast** (or 1 cake Red Star Compressed Yeast) in
	½ cup warm **water**.
Combine......	in mixing bowl
	½ cup hot scalded **milk**
	¼ cup **shortening**
	2 tablespoons **sugar** and
	1 teaspoon **salt.*** Cool to lukewarm.
Stir in........	softened yeast.
Gradually add..	2½ to 2¾ cups **Pillsbury's Best All Purpose Flour*** to form a stiff dough; beat well. (For first additions of flour, use mixer.)
Let rise.......	in warm place (85° to 90° F.) until light and doubled in size, 1 to 1½ hours.
Knead........	one-fourth of dough about 1 minute. Shape into a ball.
Divide........	remaining dough in half. Knead
	½ cup shredded **Cheddar cheese** into 1 part and
	2 tablespoons **dry onion soup** into other. Shape into balls. Cover; let rest 10 minutes. Shape dough into 1-inch balls. Place 3 balls (1 of each kind) in greased muffin cups. Sprinkle with **sesame seed**.
Let rise.......	in warm place until light, 30 to 45 minutes.
Bake.........	at 450° for 10 to 12 minutes until golden brown.

*For use with Pillsbury's Best Self-Rising Flour, omit salt.

BREADS | PAGE 79

Cheese Secrets

Senior Winner by Mrs. Tom Gaukel, Mukwonago, Wisconsin

BAKE at 400° for 10 to 12 minutes.   MAKES 40 rolls.

Cut..........	¼ pound **Cheddar cheese** into forty ½-inch cubes.
Soften........	1 packet **Red Star Special Active Dry Yeast** (or 1 cake Red Star Compressed Yeast) in ¼ cup warm **water**.
Combine......	in mixing bowl ¾ cup hot scalded **milk** 1 tablespoon **sugar** 3 tablespoons **shortening** and 1 teaspoon **salt**.* Cool to lukewarm. Stir in softened yeast.
Gradually add..	2½ to 3 cups **Pillsbury's Best All Purpose Flour*** to form a stiff dough.
Knead........	on floured surface until smooth and satiny, 4 to 6 minutes. (To knead, fold dough over on itself and push with palms of hands. Repeat this process rhythmically, turning dough one quarter way around each time.) Divide dough into 4 parts. Cut each part into 10 small pieces.
Wrap.........	dough around cheese cube. Seal edges well; shape into ball. Place on greased cookie sheets. Cover.
Let rise.......	in warm place (85° to 90° F.) until light and doubled in size, 45 to 60 minutes.
Bake.........	at 400° for 10 to 12 minutes until brown. Brush with 1 tablespoon **Land O'Lakes Butter**, melted; dip into ⅓ cup grated **Parmesan cheese**. Best served warm.

*For use with Pillsbury's Best Self-Rising Flour, omit salt.

Lemon Raisin Rolls   *Triple Treat Cloverleafs*   *Cheese Secrets*

Red Star Active Dry Yeast is softened in warm water. Lukewarm water is better for compressed yeast. To test, place a few drops of water on the inside of your wrist. Warm water feels just slightly warm; lukewarm water will feel neither warm nor cold.

Use only fresh yeast for best bread baking. The date on the back of the packet of dry yeast is the expiration date. Compressed yeast should be gray-white and crumble easily in the fingers.

A ⅔-oz. cake of compressed yeast is equal to 1 packet dry yeast.

To make dinner rolls from Cheese Secrets, cut twenty 1-inch cubes of cheese. Divide each quarter of dough into 5 pieces. Makes 20.

Best served warm. To reheat, wrap in foil and place in a 350° oven 10 to 15 minutes.

Butterflake Herb Loaf

Senior Best of Class Winner by Mrs. Roy Knighton, Chama, New Mexico

BAKE at 350° for 20 to 25 minutes.　　　　　　　　　MAKES 2 loaves.

Soften........	2 packets **Red Star Special Active Dry Yeast** (or 2 cakes Red Star Compressed Yeast) in ¼ cup warm **water**.
Combine......	in mixing bowl ⅓ cup **shortening** ¼ cup **sugar** 1 tablespoon **salt*** and 1 cup hot scalded **milk**. Cool to lukewarm.
Blend in......	2 unbeaten **eggs** and the softened yeast.
Gradually add..	4½ to 5 cups **Pillsbury's Best All Purpose Flour*** to form a stiff dough.
Knead........	on floured surface until smooth and satiny, 2 to 3 minutes. Place in greased bowl. Cover.
Let rise.......	in warm place (85° to 90° F.) until light and doubled in size, about 1½ hours. Prepare Herb Butter.
Roll out.......	half of dough on lightly floured surface to ¹⁄₁₆ to ⅛-inch thickness. Cut into 5-inch rounds with coffee can cover. Spread each round with Herb Butter; fold in half. Place on greased cookie sheet. Spread top side with Herb Butter. Continue making and folding rounds. Place on preceeding round, folded side down, overlapping three quarters of the way, to make a rectangular loaf. Repeat with remaining dough. Sprinkle with **poppy or sesame seed**.
Let rise.......	in warm place until light, 30 to 45 minutes.
Bake.........	at 350° for 20 to 25 minutes. Best served warm.

*For use with Pillsbury's Best Self-Rising Flour, omit salt.

Herb Butter

Combine ½ cup soft Land O'Lakes Butter, ½ teaspoon caraway seed, ½ teaspoon sweet basil, ½ teaspoon grated onion, ¼ teaspoon oregano, ⅛ teaspoon cayenne pepper and 1 clove garlic, minced; mix thoroughly.

BREADS | PAGE 81

Crispy Onion Snacks

Senior Winner by Mrs. Carl L. Johnson, Pompton Plains, New Jersey

BAKE at 400° for 7 to 10 minutes.   MAKES about 4 to 5 dozen.

Combine......	2 cups sifted **Pillsbury's Best All Purpose Flour*** and 1 package (1⅜ oz.) **dry onion soup** in mixing bowl.
Cut in........	½ cup **Land O'Lakes Butter** and ⅓ cup (3-oz. pkg.) **cream cheese** until particles are fine.
Combine......	1 slightly beaten **egg** with 2 tablespoons **water**. Sprinkle over flour mixture while stirring with fork until dough is moist enough to hold together. If necessary, add additional water.
Shape........	into balls, using a scant teaspoonful for each. Place on ungreased cookie sheet. Flatten to 1/16-inch thickness with bottom of glass, which has been dipped in flour. Sprinkle with **salt**.
Bake.........	at 400° for 7 to 10 minutes until light golden brown.

*Pillsbury's Best Self-Rising Flour may be substituted.

For main dish tart shells, roll out dough to 1/16 to 1/8-inch thickness. Cut into 4½-inch rounds. Shape over backs of muffin cups. Bake. Makes 24. Suggested filling, Sea King Dinner, page 14.

For crackers, cut into 2-inch squares. Serve with a soup or a chip dip.

Cottage Cheese Sticks

Junior Winner by Margaret Page Godsey, Cumberland, Virginia

BAKE at 425° for 10 to 15 minutes.   MAKES about 3 dozen.

Sift together...	into mixing bowl 1 cup sifted **Pillsbury's Best All Purpose Flour*** 1 teaspoon **salt** and ½ teaspoon double-acting **baking powder**.
Cut in........	⅓ cup **Land O'Lakes Butter** until particles are fine.
Stir in........	½ cup creamed **cottage cheese**. Form into a ball.
Roll out......	on floured surface to a 12-inch square. Brush with **milk**. Sprinkle with **celery seed**.
Cut..........	into 4x1-inch strips. Place on greased cookie sheets.
Bake.........	at 425° for 10 to 15 minutes until light golden brown.

*For use with Pillsbury's Best Self-Rising Flour, omit salt and baking powder.

BREADS

Honey Almond Brunch Cake

Mandarin Coffee Cake

Honey Almond Brunch Cake

Senior Winner by Mrs. Vincent Matheis, Chicago, Illinois

BAKE at 350° for 25 to 30 minutes.   MAKES 9-inch square coffee cake.

Sift together...	2 cups sifted **Pillsbury's Best All Purpose Flour*** 3 tablespoons **sugar** and 1 teaspoon **salt** into mixing bowl.
Cut in........	¼ cup **Land O'Lakes Butter** until particles are fine.
Soften........	1 packet **Red Star Special Active Dry Yeast** (or 1 cake Red Star Compressed Yeast) in ¼ cup warm **water**.
Combine......	1 unbeaten **egg** ¼ cup **evaporated milk or light cream** 1 teaspoon **Burnett's Almond Extract** and softened yeast. Add to dry ingredients; mix well. Cover.
Let rise.......	in warm place (85° to 90° F.) until light and doubled in size, about 1½ hours.
Combine......	in small saucepan ¼ cup **sugar** ¼ cup **Land O'Lakes Butter** and 2 tablespoons **honey**; bring to a boil. Remove from heat.
Stir in........	⅓ cup blanched **almonds**, chopped ¼ cup quick-cooking **rolled oats** and ¼ cup **evaporated milk or light cream**; blend well. Cool.
Spread.......	dough in well-greased 9-inch square pan. Spoon honey topping over dough.
Let rise.......	in warm place until light, 40 to 50 minutes.
Bake.........	at 350° for 25 to 30 minutes until golden brown. Cool. Cut coffee cake in half horizontally to make two layers. Fill. (For a firm Filling cover and store in refrigerator.)

**For use with Pillsbury's Best Self-Rising Flour, omit salt.*

Almond Butter Cream Filling

Combine 2 tablespoons flour and ½ cup milk in small saucepan. Cook, stirring constantly, until thick. Cool. Cream ¼ cup Land O'Lakes Butter, ¼ cup shortening and ½ cup sugar until fluffy. Add flour mixture and ¼ to ½ teaspoon Burnett's Almond Extract. Beat until very light.

Mandarin Coffee Cake

Senior Winner by Mrs. Melba Von Behren, St. Louis, Missouri

BAKE at 350° for 40 to 45 minutes.   MAKES 9-inch square cake.

Drain........	1 can (11 oz.) **mandarin oranges**.
Sift together...	2 cups sifted **Pillsbury's Best All Purpose Flour*** and 1 cup **sugar** into mixing bowl.
Cut in........	½ cup **Land O'Lakes Butter** until particles are fine. Reserve ½ cup crumb mixture for topping.

Italian Supper Loaf

Add..........	2½ teaspoons double-acting **baking powder** and 1 teaspoon **salt** to remaining crumb mixture.
Combine.......	¾ cup **milk** 1 teaspoon **Burnett's Pure Vanilla** and 1 unbeaten **egg**. Add to dry ingredients; mix well.
Turn..........	into 9x9 or 11x7-inch pan, well greased and lightly floured on the bottom.
Arrange.......	orange sections in rows over top of cake.
Add..........	½ teaspoon **nutmeg** to crumbs; sprinkle over oranges.
Bake..........	at 350° for 40 to 45 minutes until cake springs back when touched lightly in center.

*For use with Pillsbury's Best Self-Rising Flour, omit baking powder and salt.

Flavor variation: Sprinkle ½ cup crumbled crisp bacon or cooked pork sausage over cheese before rolling up.

Italian Supper Loaf

Senior Winner by Mrs. T. Biancorosso, Montebello, California

BAKE at 400° for 20 to 25 minutes.   MAKES 1.

Cook..........	2 cups thinly sliced **potatoes** (2 medium) in ⅓ cup **cooking oil** in skillet, turning occasionally, 10 minutes.
Add..........	¾ cup thinly sliced **onion** (1 medium); continue cooking and turning 10 minutes. Remove from heat.
Stir in........	¾ cup (6-oz. can) **tomato paste** 1 teaspoon **sugar** and 1 teaspoon **salt**; mix well. Cool completely.
Sift together...	into mixing bowl 2¼ cups sifted **Pillsbury's Best All Purpose Flour*** 3 teaspoons double-acting **baking powder** 1 teaspoon **salt**
Combine.......	¼ cup **cooking oil** with ¾ cup **milk**. Add to dry ingredients. Stir until dough clings together. Knead lightly on floured surface 10 times.
Roll out.......	on floured waxed paper to a 14x12-inch rectangle. Spread filling over dough to within ½ inch of edges.
Sprinkle with..	1 cup shredded **Cheddar cheese** and 2 tablespoons grated **Parmesan or Romano cheese**. Roll up, starting with 14-inch side. Seal edge and ends. Place, seam-side down, on ungreased cookie sheet. Prick top; brush with **milk**.
Bake..........	at 400° for 20 to 25 minutes until golden brown. Serve, cut in thin slices, hot or cold.

*For use with Pillsbury's Best Self-Rising Flour, omit baking powder and salt.

BREADS

Sunny-Side-Up Rolls

Senior Winner by Mrs. Clyde Ferrell, Long Beach, California

BAKE at 375° for 25 to 30 minutes. MAKES 15 rolls.

Soften........	2 packets **Red Star Special Active Dry Yeast** (or 2 cakes Red Star Compressed Yeast) in
	¼ cup warm **water**.
Combine......	in mixing bowl
	⅓ cup **sugar**
	⅓ cup **Land O'Lakes Butter**
	2 teaspoons **salt*** and
	¾ cup hot scalded **milk**. Cool to lukewarm.
Add.........	1 unbeaten **egg** and the softened yeast.
Gradually add..	3¾ to 4 cups **Pillsbury's Best All Purpose Flour*** to form a stiff dough; beat well. (For first additions of flour, use mixer.) Cover.
Let rest.......	in warm place (85° to 90° F.) for 30 minutes.
Combine......	in saucepan
	1 cup dairy **sour cream**
	¾ cup **sugar** and
	¼ cup firmly packed **brown sugar**. Bring to a boil; boil 3 minutes. Spread in greased 13x9-inch pan. Place 15 canned **apricot halves**, cut-side down, over topping.
Roll out.......	dough on floured surface to a 15x9-inch rectangle. Brush with soft **Land O'Lakes Butter**. Combine
	⅓ cup **sugar** and
	1 teaspoon **cinnamon**. Sprinkle over dough.
Roll up.......	starting with 15-inch side. Cut into 1-inch slices. Place on apricot halves. Cover.
Let rise......	in warm place until light, about 1 hour.
Bake.........	at 375° for 25 to 30 minutes until deep golden brown. Invert; let stand 2 to 3 minutes before removing pan.

*For use with Pillsbury's Best Self-Rising Flour, omit salt.

Cheese Wafer Snacks

Junior Winner by Roger Ivice, Chicago, Illinois

BAKE at 375° for 8 to 10 minutes. MAKES about 4 dozen.

Sift together...	2 cups sifted **Pillsbury's Best All Purpose Flour***
	1 cup **corn meal** and
	1½ teaspoons **salt** into mixing bowl.
Cut in........	¾ cup **Land O'Lakes Butter** until particles are fine.
Add.........	1 cup **milk**
	1 cup shredded **Cheddar cheese** and
	1 tablespoon grated **onion**; mix well.
Drop.........	by rounded teaspoonfuls onto well-greased and lightly floured cookie sheets. Spread to about 4-inch circles with wet fingers. Sprinkle with **poppy seed**.
Bake.........	at 375° for 8 to 10 minutes until light golden brown. Remove from sheets immediately.

*For use with Pillsbury's Best Self-Rising Flour, decrease salt to ½ teaspoon.

BREADS | PAGE 85

Sunny-Side-Up Rolls

Cheese Wafer Snacks

Cherry Blossoms

Other flavors of pie filling may be substituted for the cherry.

Cherry Blossoms

Senior Winner by Mrs. Marie Case, Oconomowoc, Wisconsin

BAKE at 350° for 30 to 35 minutes.   MAKES 2 coffee cakes.

Soften.......	1 packet **Red Star Special Active Dry Yeast** (or 1 cake Red Star Compressed Yeast) in ¼ cup warm **water**.
Combine......	in mixing bowl ⅓ cup **sugar** ⅓ cup **Land O'Lakes Butter** 2 teaspoons **salt*** and ½ cup hot scalded **milk**. Cool to lukewarm.
Stir in.......	2 unbeaten **eggs** and the softened yeast.
Gradually add..	3¾ to 4 cups **Pillsbury's Best All Purpose Flour*** to form a stiff dough.
Knead........	on floured surface until smooth and satiny, 5 to 7 minutes. Place in greased bowl; cover.
Let rise......	in warm place (85° to 90° F.) until light and doubled in size, 1½ to 2 hours.
Open........	1 can (1 lb. 5 oz.) **cherry pie filling**.
Roll out......	half of dough on lightly floured surface to a 24x6-inch rectangle. Spread soft **Land O'Lakes Butter** down center third. Top with half of cherry pie filling. Sprinkle ¼ cup **sugar** over cherries.
Fold.........	one side of dough over filling; fold opposite side to overlap. Seal edges. Place one end, seam-side down, in center of well-greased 9-inch round pan; wind into pan to make a flat coil. Flatten slightly. Make deep slashes from center to within ½ inch of outside edge 1 inch apart. Sprinkle with **sugar**. Cover. Repeat with remaining dough.
Let rise......	in warm place until light and doubled, about 1 hour.
Bake........	at 350° for 30 to 35 minutes until golden brown. Cool slightly. Remove from pans.

*For use with Pillsbury's Best Self-Rising Flour, omit salt.

BREADS

Sweet breads are a real conversation piece at a dessert party. Try this coffee cake at your next party.

Danish Apple Coffee Cake

Senior Winner by Mrs. Margaret Ziegenhorn, Chicago, Illinois

BAKE at 350° for 30 to 35 minutes.   MAKES 2.

Soften........ 1 packet **Red Star Special Active Dry Yeast** (or 1 cake **Red Star Compressed Yeast**) in
¼ cup warm **water**.

Combine...... 2¾ cups **Pillsbury's Best All Purpose Flour*** with
1 teaspoon **salt** in mixing bowl.

Cut in........ ½ cup **Land O'Lakes Butter** until particles are fine.

Add.......... ½ cup dairy **sour cream**
2 unbeaten **eggs** and softened yeast. Mix to form a dough. Cover. Chill at least 2 hours.

Combine...... 1 cup **sugar** and
2 teaspoons **cinnamon**. Sprinkle 2 tablespoons on rolling surface.

Roll out....... dough, half at a time, to a 12x8-inch rectangle. Sprinkle with 2 tablespoons sugar-cinnamon mixture. Fold in half. Repeat rolling and folding 2 more times, adding sugar-cinnamon as necessary. Roll out again.

Sprinkle...... 1 tablespoon **bread crumbs** down center third of rectangle. Place half of Filling over crumbs. Sprinkle with
1 tablespoon **bread crumbs**; dot with **Land O'Lakes Butter**.

Fold.......... one side of dough over Filling, then fold opposite side to overlap. Seal edges. Place, seam-side up, on greased cookie sheet. Make deep diagonal slashes across top about 3 inches apart and to within ½ inch of edge.

Let rise....... in warm place (85° to 90° F.) until light, 30 minutes.

Bake......... at 350° for 30 to 35 minutes until golden brown.

*For use with Pillsbury's Best Self-Rising Flour, omit salt.

Apple Filling

Drain 1 can (1 lb. 4 oz.) pie sliced apples on absorbent paper. Just before placing on dough, combine with ½ cup sugar, 2 teaspoons cinnamon, 1 teaspoon grated lemon rind and ¼ teaspoon nutmeg.

BREADS | PAGE 87

Unless otherwise specified in the recipe, all types of yeast breads should be removed from the pan immediately after baking. This prevents a soggy bottom crust.

Peanut-Buttery Puffs

Senior Second Prize Winner by Mrs. Donald J. Schindelholz, Beloit, Wisconsin

BAKE at 400° for 20 to 25 minutes. MAKES 12 rolls.

Cream.......... ½ cup **peanut butter** and
2 tablespoons **Land O'Lakes Butter** with
¼ cup firmly packed **brown sugar**. Set aside.

Soften......... 1 packet **Red Star Special Active Dry Yeast** (or 1 cake Red Star Compressed Yeast) in
¼ cup warm **water**.

Combine...... in mixing bowl
¾ cup **buttermilk**, heated to lukewarm
2 tablespoons **sugar**
2 tablespoons **shortening**
1½ teaspoons **salt***
2 unbeaten **eggs** and the softened yeast.

Gradually add.. 2½ to 3 cups **Pillsbury's Best All Purpose Flour*** to form a soft dough; beat well. (For first additions of flour, use mixer.)

Spoon......... one rounded teaspoonful dough into 12 well-greased muffin cups; flatten. Top each with 1 teaspoonful peanut butter mixture. Cover with remaining dough. Spread to cover filling.

Let rise....... in warm place (85° to 90° F.) until light and doubled in size, 45 to 60 minutes.

Bake.......... at 400° for 20 to 25 minutes until golden brown. Spread Topping on warm rolls.

*For use with Pillsbury's Best Self-Rising Flour, omit salt. Decrease rising time to 40 to 50 minutes.

Peanut Topping

Combine 2 tablespoons sugar, 2 tablespoons chopped peanuts and 2 tablespoons soft Land O'Lakes Butter.

Bacon-Nut Bread

Senior Winner by Mrs. William W. Lyth, Cleveland, Ohio

BAKE at 350° for 60 to 65 minutes.   MAKES 9x5-inch loaf.

Fry............	5 strips (¼ lb.) **bacon** until crisp; reserve ¼ cup drippings. Crumble bacon.
Sift together...	2 cups sifted **Pillsbury's Best All Purpose Flour*** ⅓ cup **sugar** 2½ teaspoons double-acting **baking powder** 1 teaspoon **salt**
Soften.........	⅔ cup (two 3-oz. pkgs.) **cream cheese**. Add 1 unbeaten **egg** and reserved drippings; cream well.
Gradually add..	¾ cup **milk**, beating well.
Stir in.........	¾ cup chopped **Diamond Walnuts** ¼ cup chopped **green pepper** ¼ cup chopped **onion** and bacon.
Blend in.......	dry ingredients. Stir until dry particles are moistened. Turn into 9x5x3-inch pan, greased on bottom.
Bake..........	at 350° for 60 to 65 minutes. Let stand at least 4 hours before slicing.

*Self-rising flour is not recommended for use in this recipe.

Quick Bubble Loaf

Senior Winner by Mrs. F. Taylor Grimm, Bethesda, Maryland

BAKE at 375° for 50 to 55 minutes.   MAKES 9x5-inch loaf.

Sift together...	into mixing bowl 3 cups sifted **Pillsbury's Best All Purpose Flour*** 2 tablespoons **sugar** 4½ teaspoons double-acting **baking powder** 1½ teaspoons **salt**
Cut in.........	⅓ cup **shortening** until particles are fine.
Combine.......	1 cup **milk** and 1 unbeaten **egg**. Add to dry ingredients; mix until all dry particles are moistened. Knead lightly on floured surface 12 strokes.
Roll out.......	on floured surface to a 21x12-inch rectangle. Cut into 3-inch squares. Wrap each around a packaged pitted **prune**. Shape into balls.
Dip...........	balls into ¼ cup **Land O'Lakes Butter**, melted. Roll in mixture of ½ cup chopped **Diamond Walnuts** ½ cup **sugar** and 1 teaspoon **cinnamon**. Place in greased 9x5x3-inch pan. Sprinkle remaining sugar-nut mixture over balls.
Bake..........	at 375° for 50 to 55 minutes until golden brown. Cool in pan 15 minutes; remove carefully. Cool, slice to serve. If desired, serve warm; pull off balls.

*For use with Pillsbury's Best Self-Rising Flour, omit baking powder and salt.

Doughnuts may be baked in 350° oven 12 to 15 minutes.

Tea-Time Date Doughnuts

Senior Winner by Mrs. Otto E. Kneisel, Powhattan, Kansas

FRY at 350° F. for 2 to 3 minutes. MAKES 3 dozen.

Soften........	1 packet **Red Star Special Active Dry Yeast** (or 1 cake Red Star Compressed Yeast) in ¼ cup warm **water**.
Combine......	in mixing bowl ½ cup hot scalded **milk** ¼ cup **sugar** 1 tablespoon **instant tea** 1 tablespoon grated **orange rind** 3 tablespoons **Land O'Lakes Butter** ¼ cup **orange juice** and 1 teaspoon **salt**.* Cool to lukewarm.
Blend in......	1 unbeaten **egg** and the softened yeast.
Gradually add..	3 to 3½ cups **Pillsbury's Best All Purpose Flour*** to form a stiff dough.
Knead........	on floured surface until smooth and satiny, 3 to 5 minutes. Place in greased bowl; cover.
Let rise.......	in warm place (85° to 90° F.) until light and doubled in size, 45 to 60 minutes.
Roll out.......	dough on lightly floured surface to about ¼-inch thickness. Cut into 2½-inch rounds. Place 1 teaspoonful Filling in center. Moisten edges. Fold in half; seal.
Let rise.......	in warm place until light, about 30 minutes.
Combine......	2 cups sifted **confectioners' sugar** 1 to 2 tablespoons hot **water** and ¼ teaspoon **Burnett's Maple Flavor**.
Fry..........	in hot deep fat (350° F.) about 1 minute on each side. Frost warm with maple glaze. (If desired, omit glaze and coat with confectioners' sugar.)

*For use with Pillsbury's Best Self-Rising Flour, omit salt.

Date Filling

Combine in saucepan 1 cup finely cut dates, ½ cup finely chopped Diamond Walnuts, ⅓ cup confectioners' sugar and ⅓ cup water. Cook over medium heat, stirring constantly, until thick.

Bacon-Nut Bread

Quick Bubble Loaf

Tea-Time Date Doughnuts

Any flavor of preserves desired may be used. For a real European touch, frost warm Coffee Cake with a confectioners' sugar glaze.

Hungarian Jubilee Bread

Senior Winner by Mrs. Edith Racz, Denver, Colorado

BAKE at 350° for 40 to 45 minutes.   MAKES 13x9-inch coffee cake.

Soften........ 1 packet **Red Star Special Active Dry Yeast** (or 1 cake Red Star Compressed Yeast) in
¼ cup warm **water**.

Cut.......... ¾ cup soft **Land O'Lakes Butter** into
4 cups sifted **Pillsbury's Best All Purpose Flour*** until particles are fine. Make a well in center.

Add.......... ¾ cup hot scalded **milk**, cooled to lukewarm.
¼ cup **sugar**
1 unbeaten **egg**
1½ teaspoons **salt** and the softened yeast. Mix thoroughly to form a stiff dough. Cover.

Let rise....... in warm place (85° to 90° F.) until light and doubled in size, 45 to 60 minutes.

Combine...... 1 cup **raspberry or strawberry preserves** with
2 to 3 drops **Burnett's Red Food Coloring**.

Chop........ 1 cup (4-oz. can) **Diamond Walnuts** (reserve 2 tablespoons for topping).

Divide........ dough into 4 parts. Roll out one part to a 15x11-inch rectangle. Fit into a 13x9-inch pan, allowing excess to hang over sides of pan. Spread ⅓ cup of the preserves over bottom; sprinkle with ⅓ cup walnuts.

Roll out....... second portion of dough to a 13x9-inch rectangle. Place in pan. Spread with ⅓ cup preserves and sprinkle with ⅓ cup walnuts. Repeat with remaining dough, leaving top layer plain. Fold sides over coffee cake and flute. Prick with fork.

Bake......... at 350° for 40 to 45 minutes until golden brown. Remove from pan immediately. Brush with soft **Land O'Lakes Butter**. Combine reserved nuts and
2 tablespoons **confectioners' sugar**. Sprinkle over coffee cake. Cool. To serve, cut into thin slices.

*For use with Pillsbury's Best Self-Rising Flour, omit salt.

Maple Nut Cinnamon Rolls

Junior First Prize Winner by Mary Bea Mantz, Wolf Creek, Montana

BAKE at 350° for 30 to 35 minutes.   MAKES 2 dozen.

Soften........	1 packet **Red Star Special Active Dry Yeast** (or 1 cake Red Star Compressed Yeast) in ¼ cup warm **water**.
Combine......	in mixing bowl 1 cup quick-cooking **rolled oats** ¾ cup hot scalded **milk** ½ cup **shortening** ⅓ cup firmly packed **brown sugar** and 1½ teaspoons **salt**.* Cool to lukewarm.
Blend in......	2 unbeaten **eggs** and the softened yeast.
Gradually add..	3½ to 4 cups **Pillsbury's Best All Purpose Flour*** to form a stiff dough; beat well. Cover.
Let rise.......	in warm place (85° to 90° F.) until light and doubled in size, about 1½ hours.
Combine......	in 13x9-inch pan ½ cup **maple flavored syrup** ¼ cup firmly packed **brown sugar** ¼ cup **Land O'Lakes Butter**, melted 1 tablespoon water and ¼ teaspoon **Burnett's Maple Flavor**, if desired. Add ⅔ cup chopped **Diamond Walnuts**.
Roll out.......	dough on floured surface to 24x12-inch rectangle. Brush with ¼ cup **Land O'Lakes Butter**, melted.
Combine......	⅔ cup firmly packed **brown sugar** 1 tablespoon grated **orange rind** and 1 teaspoon **cinnamon**. Sprinkle over dough. Roll up, starting with 24-inch side. Cut into 1-inch slices; place in prepared pan.
Let rise......	in warm place until light and doubled, about 1 hour.
Bake.........	at 350° for 30 to 35 minutes until golden brown. Cool 1 minute; invert onto serving plate or wire rack.

*For use with Pillsbury's Best Self-Rising Flour, omit salt.

Rolls may be baked in muffin cups. Omit chopped walnuts and place 3 Diamond Walnut Halves in the bottom of each cup. Decrease baking time to 25 to 30 minutes.

BREADS

Creamy Chive Rings

Senior Winner by Mrs. Vincent R. Costanzi, Chisholm, Minnesota

BAKE at 350° for 20 to 25 minutes. MAKES 2.

Soften......... 1 packet **Red Star Special Active Dry Yeast** (or 1 cake Red Star Compressed Yeast) in
¼ cup warm **water**.

Combine....... in mixing bowl
⅓ cup **sugar**
⅓ cup **shortening**
¼ cup **Pillsbury Mashed Potato Flakes**
1½ teaspoons **salt*** and
1 cup hot scalded **milk**. Cool to lukewarm.

Stir in......... 1 unbeaten **egg** and the softened yeast.

Gradually add..3½ to 4 cups **Pillsbury's Best All Purpose Flour*** to form a stiff dough.

Knead......... on lightly floured surface until smooth and satiny, 5 to 8 minutes. (To knead, fold dough over on itself and push with palms of hands. Repeat this process rhythmically, turning dough one quarter way around each time.) Place in greased bowl; cover.

Let rise........ in warm place (85° to 90° F.) until light and doubled in size, 1 to 1½ hours.

Divide......... dough in half. Roll out on lightly floured surface to a 16x12-inch rectangle. Spread with half of Filling.

Roll up........ starting with 16-inch side. Cut into 1-inch slices. Overlap slices on greased cookie sheet to make an oval ring. Repeat with remaining dough.

Let rise........ in warm place until light and doubled, about 1 hour.

Bake.......... at 350° for 20 to 25 minutes until golden brown.

*For use with Pillsbury's Best Self-Rising Flour, omit salt.

Chive Filling

Combine 1 slightly beaten egg, ¾ cup heavy cream, ⅓ cup finely chopped chives or green onion tops and ½ teaspoon salt in top of double boiler. Cook over boiling water until thick.

An easy trick for cutting rolls is to use a heavy sewing thread. Place thread under dough; bring ends of thread up and around sides of dough. Cross as if to tie, cutting dough into slices.

INDEX | PAGE NUMBERS

Main Dishes

BEEF BURGER BAR-B-QUE..........11
Teen specialty—onion flavored buns baked on top of a barbeque hamburger filling.

CHICKEN CURRY CROQUETTES......13
Savory croquettes are batter dipped then fried and served with a creamy sauce.

CHICKEN DELISH................17
Chicken, ham and mushrooms smothered with a creamy chicken sauce.

CORNED BEEF WHEELS............16
Spicy corned beef is baked inside pinwheel biscuits. A sour cream tomato sauce makes the dish complete.

HIDDEN CHEESEBURGERS..........19
Cheese filled hamburgers are baked inside each bun.

HOT CHEESE PUPS...............15
A Saturday night special—cheese filled yeast rolls fried in butter.

HUNGRY BOYS' CASSEROLE........ 7
A prize-winning hamburger and bean casserole with a special biscuit topping.

ITALIAN PANCAKE CASSEROLE......12
Lasagne-like casserole layered with herb pancakes, hamburger, tomatoes and cheeses. Excellent for a crowd.

PARTY PORK BARBECUE........... 9
Pork shoulder baked in a sweet-sour sauce—topped with mushroom biscuits.

PENNSYLVANIA KNOCKBOCKLE......14
A frankfurter-vegetable casserole topped with tender cheese biscuits.

SEA KING DINNER...............14
Company fare—shrimp and crab meat combined in a savory white sauce with a touch of cheese on top.

SUNDAY SUPPER FOLDOVERS.......10
Last minute idea! Flaky pastry is wrapped around a corned beef hash filling.

SWEET CHERRY HAM BAKE.........18
Rich delicate Parkerhouse biscuits top this cherry ham casserole.

VENETIAN VEAL PIE.............8
A veal pie with a pizza flavor is covered with a layer of cheese and herb pastry.

Cakes

ANGEL SQUARES.................26
An all American cake—a creamy butter frosting and cashews surround this easy moist angel type cake.

BROWN VELVET CAKE.............35
Velvety chocolate layers with a creamy peanut filling and chocolate frosting.

BUTTERSCOTCH SUNDAE TREAT.....31
A crown cake with a pineapple-cherry topping.

CHERRY ALMOND FUDGE CAKE.....33
Double good—cherry pie filling goes in the cake as well as between the layers.

CHERRY MARBLE CAKE............34
Chocolate is marbled through a cherry-walnut cake. The frosting is chocolate, too.

CHOCOLATE CELEBRATION CAKE....24
A real party cake—three layered chocolate cake speckled with chocolate pieces.

CINNAMON TOAST CAKE...........28
An easy to make quick-mix cake with butter, sugar and cinnamon topping.

ICE CREAM CAKE................38
Ice cream, vanilla pudding and coffee are combined for a new flavor in cake.

IMPERIAL CROWN CAKE...........36
The crowning touch to a successful meal—moist chocolate-butterscotch cake with a special frosting and topping.

JAMAICAN MYSTERY CAKE.........32
Here's the mystery—a new easy way to make a coffee marble cake.

KENTUCKY BUTTER CAKE..........25
A rich pound cake made extra moist with a butter sauce.

LEMON BUTTER LAYERS...........27
Lemon pound cake made festive with its creamy lemon filling and nut crunch topping.

OLD TIME CHOCOLATE CAKE.......38
Chocolate and oatmeal are combined to make a dark, moist fudge cake.

PEANUT BUTTER AND JELLY CAKE..37
Favorite flavors are combined in this all-occasion cake.

PLANTATION PRIDE CAKE.........30
This brown sugar cake has a hint of chocolate and a broiled-on topping.

ROCKY ROAD NUT CAKE...........22
Chewy loaf cake topped with a marshmallow and butterscotch glaze.

SWEET APPLETS.................23
Spicy apple cupcakes rolled in sugar-cinnamon for a quick coffee special.

TROPICAL ORANGE CAKE..........22
The new touch in date cake is the candied orange pieces.

UPSIDE DOWN PENUCHE CAKE.....29
Easy all-in-one cake. Coconut-brown sugar mixture is baked under a moist yellow cake.

WALNUT GLORY CAKE.............21
Walnuts and cinnamon add flavor and crunch to this extra delicate sponge cake.

INDEX

Cookies

ALMOND TOSCA BARS..............50
A buttery bar with a surprise chocolate layer and a creamy almond topping.

APPLE HARVEST SQUARES..........43
Apples, nuts and coconut make this bar unique. Serve as a cookie or a dessert.

BUTTER CRUNCH SLICES...........42
A butterscotch-peanut butter center enhances this rich refrigerator cookie.

BUTTERSCOTCH PINWHEELS........46
Just like candy! A fudge base rolled up around a butterscotch filling.

CANDY SURPRISES................53
Brown sugar bars with a surprise layer of peanut butter and milk chocolate.

CHOCOLATE BEAU CATCHERS.......47
Kids will love them—a chocolate-date cookie with a browned butter icing.

CHOCOLATE PILLOWS..............47
Milk chocolate candy bar pieces are baked between strips of spritz cookies.

CHOCOLATE SHADOWS.............54
An eye catcher! Chocolate is swirled through a peanut butter cookie.

CRUNCHY DATE SLICES............44
Peanut crunch adds a new touch to this no-bake chocolate date roll.

FROSTED FRUIT JUMBLES..........44
New for the holidays! Candied fruit cookies topped with a lemon glaze.

FUDGE NOUGATS..................41
A real favorite—an easy no-bake fudge cookie that tastes like candy.

GINGER BOYS....................51
Swiss cookies with an American touch—made especially for the kids.

LEMON-Y LAYERS.................46
Just like a dream bar—new with a twist of lemon.

LONG AGO LEMON COOKIES........45
Plump sour cream cookies with a hint of lemon.

MACAROONIES...................50
Chocolate morsels make these chewy macaroon cookies different.

MACAROON POLKA DOTS..........43
A chewy coconut bar with chocolate morsels hidden inside.

ORANGE-OATMEAL CHEWS........53
The all-time favorite chewy oatmeal cookie with a touch of orange.

ORIENTAL TREASURE COOKIES......42
A chewy brown sugar snap made with an unusual almond topping.

PEANUT BUTTER CRUNCHIES.......54
Crispy chow mein noodles add crunch to a peanut butter-marshmallow bar.

PEANUT DRUM COOKIES...........52
Peanut cookies, stacked in 3's with vanilla filling, then covered with chocolate frosting.

PEPPERMINT TWISTS..............52
A clever way to make candy canes—just 2 colors of dough and a cookie press.

SPICICLES......................45
Try these rich fruit sticks for variety on your cookie plate.

SPICY CRINKLES.................55
A cookie jar favorite—spice and rum flavored drop cookies.

TWIN CINNAMON WHIRLS..........55
Crisp cinnamon coated cookies rolled into double swirls.

WALNUT SANDWICH COOKIES......51
An orange filling and topping enhances a butter cookie.

Pies

APPLE ÁLA CREAM PIE............65
Apples baked in a custard sauce. A crumb topping completes the pie.

APPLE 'N CHEESE TARTS..........63
A real favorite—cheese pastry hides an apple-raisin filling.

BECKY'S FRUIT PIE..............64
An old-fashioned fruit pie topped with a fluffy cinnamon meringue.

BONANZA BANANA PIE............61
A delicious, fluffy banana chiffon pie chilled to perfection!

FRENCH PEAR PIE................62
A unique party pie—pears topped with ginger-flavored sour cream and brown sugar.

LITTLE SURPRISE PIES...........62
Chocolate wafers are hidden between a coconut-rum topping and a butter crust.

MELBA STREUSEL PIE............59
Peaches and raspberries combine with a streusel topping for a year-round pie.

MOCHA FRAPPE PIE..............60
A velvety two-layered chocolate pie in a rich flaky crust.

ORANGE DREAM PIE..............57
A touch of orange and a different method make this chiffon cheese pie special.

PINEAPPLE BRULÉ PIE............58
A broiled pineapple coconut topping gives custard pie a new touch.

SOUTHERN PINEAPPLE TARTS......63
Pecan pie flavored with pineapple. You bake them as little pies.

Desserts

APPLE DESSERT PANCAKES........71
A delicate orange topping flavors these apple filled crepes.

CHOCOLATE CREAM TORTE........73
An elegant dessert. Coconut meringue layers are stacked together with a rich chocolate filling.

INDEX PAGE 95

EASY HAWAIIAN TORTE............72
This moist pineapple cake with its baked-on brown sugar-coconut topping is delicious with ice cream.

PINEAPPLE DESSERT PIE............69
Pineapple-whipped cream goes between and on top of this easy unique dessert.

RASPBERRY CONTINENTAL..........70
A make-ahead dessert with a luscious raspberry and butter cream filling.

RHUBARB DESSERT DUMPLINGS....68
A family dessert—fluffy dumplings top a cinnamon flavored rhubarb sauce.

SUNDAY SPECIAL TORTE...........67
A three layer raspberry meringue torte filled with sour cream.

Quick Breads

BACON-NUT BREAD................88
Crisp bacon bits and green pepper add color and flavor to this bread.

CHEESE WAFER SNACKS...........84
Delightful cheese rounds, eat them with soup or serve as a snack.

COTTAGE CHEESE STICKS.........81
Cottage cheese is added to a buttery pastry to make a snack stick.

CRISPY ONION SNACKS............81
Two favorites—dry onion soup and cream cheese are combined to make this snack cracker.

EUROPEAN COFFEE CAKE..........76
A layer of sour cream makes this cherry kuchen extra good.

ITALIAN SUPPER LOAF.............83
A biscuit dough rolled around a spicy tomato and potato filling. Serve with a salad for a complete meal.

MANDARIN COFFEE CAKE..........82
A coffee cake with a golden glow of mandarin orange slices on the top.

QUICK BUBBLE LOAF..............88
In each bubble is a prune—each bubble is rolled in a cinnamon-sugar mixture.

Yeast Breads

BUTTERFLAKE HERB LOAF.........80
An herb butter separates each slice. Just pull off slices as you eat.

CHEESE SECRETS.................79
These small rolls with cheese centers are excellent to serve with soup.

CHERRY BLOSSOMS...............85
Cherry pie filling peeks through this sparkling coffee cake.

CREAMY CHIVE RINGS............92
Rolls swirled with a creamy chive filling are shaped into a large dinner ring.

DAISY BREAKFAST CAKE..........77
Shaping that's easy and unusual makes these fruit filled coffee cakes distinctive.

DANISH APPLE COFFEE CAKE.......86
A flaky coffee cake coated with cinnamon-sugar and filled with apples.

HONEY ALMOND BRUNCH CAKE....82
A honey almond kuchen split and filled with almond butter cream.

HUNGARIAN JUBILEE BREAD.......90
Layers of bread, nuts and jam are all baked together to make a ribbon bread.

LEMON RAISIN ROLLS.............78
Cottage cheese, lemon and raisins flavor a yeast puff.

MAPLE NUT CINNAMON ROLLS.....91
Oatmeal and maple flavored syrup make a unique cinnamon roll.

PEACH FLIP......................74
Jam and a sugar-cinnamon mixture are rolled up in this coffee cake which flips open during baking.

PEANUT-BUTTERY PUFFS..........87
These batter rolls have a spoonful of peanut butter in the center.

SUNNY-SIDE-UP ROLLS............84
Sour cream and apricots provide a different topping for the popular cinnamon rolls.

TEA-TIME DATE DOUGHNUTS.......89
Tea adds interest to a date filled doughnut which may be baked or fried.

TRIPLE TREAT CLOVERLEAFS........78
A different flavor in each "leaf" makes this roll extra special.

Frostings and Fillings

BROWN VELVET FROSTING..........35
BROWNED BUTTER FROSTING.......47
BUTTER FROSTING................26
BUTTERSCOTCH COCONUT FROSTING......................38
BUTTERSCOTCH ICING.............22
CHOCOLATE CREAM CHEESE FROSTING......................33
CHOCOLATE FROSTING............24
CREAMY PEANUT FILLING..........35
FLUFFY FROSTING................37
FUDGE FROSTING.................34
HONEY CHOCOLATE FROSTING.....39
LEMON CREAM FILLING...........27
ORANGE COCONUT FROSTING......22
RUM CREAM FILLING.............32
SEA FOAM FROSTING.............36
SPICY BUTTER FROSTING..........45

the most useful cook book you'll ever use!

At last, a family cook book based on the way modern families really live!

The Family Cook Book is the one book you will turn to 365 days a year. Traditional recipes for family favorites, short and simple ideas using convenience foods, and recipes with a gourmet flavor, highlight each chapter of this book.

From a nationwide recipe search, we gathered the actual recipes that families love best—each one carefully tested by a highly qualified staff of 28 home economists. We also looked for—and found—recipes that save time, save steps and save money.

HANDY WIRE RACK—FREE
Fits compactly right into the ring bound book. Just snap it on and you have a sturdy reading stand.

20 big chapters, with these features:

MEAT, GAME & POULTRY — How to make them tender, juicy, and tasty. New recipes for game and game birds. Tips on buying. Meat cookery timetables, "How To Carve" illustrations.

V. I. P. COOKERY — Plan Ahead Recipes — fun for you as well as your guests. Color Schemes. Suggested menus and recipes for buffet dinners, brunches, patio parties.

LUNCHEON AND SUPPER DISHES—"Make Ahead" recipes for busy homemakers. Hearty dishes for hungry teenagers and the man in your life. Interesting ways to turn leftovers into planned-overs.

OUTDOOR COOKING — How to put extra zest into outdoor meals with mouth-watering aroma of charcoal broiled or roasted meat, and new ideas for the grill from appetizers to "meals on a stick" to grilled desserts.

CREATIVE COOKERY — Be creative, colorful, and cosmopolitan with appetizers, short and simple, or elaborate. Add a special touch to every meal with hot breads. Nothing compares with a plump crusty loaf of freshly baked bread or rolls, whether you do it from scratch or get a headstart with mixes or refrigerated dough.

PUT A LIFT INTO MEALS WITH SEASONINGS—44 herbs, spices, and seasonings with suggestions for use with 33 meats, fish, and vegetables—all made easy in chart form.

SEND NO MONEY—Simply fill in the attached post card and drop it in the mailbox — no postage required. When the Family Cook Book arrives, look it over first. We're sure you'll be pleased, but if you're not, simply return it to us within ten days and you'll owe us nothing.

1,898 KITCHEN-TESTED RECIPES • 576 PAGES—20 SECTIONS • $4.95 RING-BOUND ... $3.95 REGULAR